the me book

the
me
book

An Illustrated Manual for Being Human

by Susan Collins

ROUNDTABLE PUBLISHING, INC.
SANTA MONICA   CALIFORNIA

ROUNDTABLE PUBLISHING, INC.
933 Pico Boulevard
Santa Monica, CA 90405

Copyright © 1983 in manuscript by Susan Collins

First Printing, 1986

Library of Congress Catalog Card Number—84-060763

PRINTED IN THE UNITED STATES OF AMERICA

CONTENTS

FOREWORD

Like life, this book is deceptively simple. For those of you, like me, who usually dive right into the middle of things, or rush through to get to the end, this book, like life, must begin at the beginning. And some things have to happen before other things make sense. That's just the way it is.

I bring a lot, my whole life, to share with you. This book is not really about what I say. It's about what you see about what I say. It is a mirror I hold up for you to look into. The details of my life are unique, and yet, underneath, like it or not, my life is like yours.

And oh yes, this book, like life, didn't match my pictures. I was surprised at first, but my story didn't fit into the usual form of a book.

Who am I, Susan Collins, and why am I writing this book? Since I was little, I have been searching for those who could tell me about life, looking always outside for what I now know was within already. In my search I found lots of things I wished I had learned about in school, things I wished had been in books. But those things weren't there. I wanted a sort of manual for how to be me, how to operate my life, not an encyclopedia of how to be like others, though that was what I usually found.

My experience has been thorough:

> childhood at home, figuring out my parents;
>
> elementary school, figuring out my teachers;
>
> high school, figuring out my friends;
>
> college, living away, confused about me and dissatisfied with the "degreed upon" answers;
>
> marriage, trying to make my husband play his part the way I thought he should;
>
> motherhood, playing out my ideas of being a parent, trying to do it right;

and finally a single mother, alone with my fears and doubts, at last discovering just how capable I truly was, all along.

I searched for the truth in others' ideas, participated fully in TM, est, and Insight Seminars. I read. I lived. And through it all, I grew to know *I knew*. I had learned enough, done enough to be able to look deeply inside, listen carefully inside, and create a guidebook, the kind of manual I wished I'd had growing up and going through life.

This book is not just for me. I give it now to you, so you may discover the *me* in you.

I love you.

—Susan Collins

the me book

1

To my parents:
How I created me, as told by the infant me

me: I am all there is,
everything.
I can think anything I want,
feel anything I want,
do anything I want.

Until one day.
I'm hungry and I'm not getting to eat.
I'm all wet too. What's going on?
I've never felt like this before.
Look at this. I'm in this little body.

It can't do much.
I can't do much.

I can't even do the things I need to do
to take care of me, feed me, change me.
I'm not powerful at all!
My heavens, I'm helpless!
Something's gone wrong.
There must be something else,
someone else besides me,
someone who can do what I can't do.

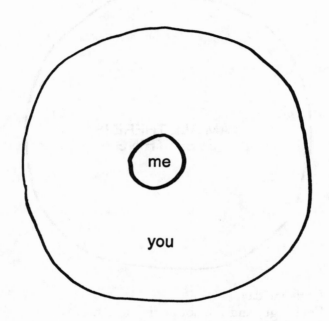

You,
you can do what I can't do.
You can do everything else.
I need you to do what I can't do.
But where are you?
Why aren't you doing what I need?
Aren't you like me?
Aren't you a part of me?

So my discovery process begins.
How do I get you out there
to feed me, move me, change me?

Wait a minute. I'm wet again.
How do I get you to do the things
I can't do?
What'll I do first?
I'll try smiling and cooing.
That seems easy enough.
I'll even bang on my crib a little.
Ah, it worked. Here you come.
Good. I'm hungry.
Here goes, umm.

It works. You are a part of me.
So as a successful smiler,
I smile and get my needs met.
My system number one for how to get what I need
is smile, coo, and bang on the crib,
and you will come and take care of me.
It works. I am a happy baby!
You do what I need.
With you, I can do it all again.

Until one day.
What's up? Something's gone wrong again.
I've been smiling and cooing for hours.
I even kicked my crib halfway across the room
and you haven't come.
What's going on? What's wrong with you?
I don't like this.
I'm upset. No, I'm mad. No, I hurt.
I'm gonna cry, whah!
I mean I'm really going to cry.
This is a disaster!

My system doesn't work.
The only thing I know how to do
to get what I need from you doesn't work,
and I'm hungry!
This crying takes a lot of effort.
I'm exhausted.
Hey wait, you're coming.
Ah, food at last.
Crying works too!

Smiling, cooing, banging on the crib
worked for a while,
but it doesn't always work.
I have to expand my system.
Sometimes smiling, cooing, and banging works,
and sometimes crying works too.
I am making decisions about life.
I am deciding about me, about my system,
what I have to do to get what I need,
or rather what I have to do to get *you*
to do what I need.

Here you come.
I like it when you come.
I feel whole with you.
I like the things you do for me.
You feed me, you bathe me, you play with me.
Oh, look, you are picking me up.

But what is this down here—the floor?
It's hard.

What is this all about?
Hey look, I can do something on my own!
This body I'm in is starting to work.
I can rock back and forth.
I can even get it moving
if I push with this knee a little.
Things are changing.
But wait, LOOK AT THAT!
What is THAT? I want THAT!
Here I go.

NO. (SLAP!)

Ouch!
Wow, that hurt!
The game has expanded.
There are new rules outside my crib.

I want THAT, and wham!
That smarts. I'd better be careful what I want.
I'm moving out into your territory now.
I'd better find out what your rules are
before I get into more trouble.
I guess you'll let me know.
What did you say? *NO.* Maybe that's a clue.

I felt safer in my crib. It was getting a little tight,
but it wasn't so dangerous.
Hold on, I'm talking too much.

I'd better pay more attention.
Being wrong is painful!

So here we are. Let's look at a
time lapse summary of what keeps happening.
This is how it all began.
I was all there is, everything.
I was hungry, I ate.
Wet, I was dried—
though maybe not exactly when I wanted it—
until the day I wanted THAT!

You: *NO.* (SLAP!)
    You can't have that.

  me: Why not?

You: That's dangerous! That will hurt you.
  me: Oh, hurt?

You: Like this. (SLAP!)

  me: I don't like that, that hurts.

You: That's right. Don't you *ever* do THAT again!

me: Whew, that's dangerous.
I can't do that.

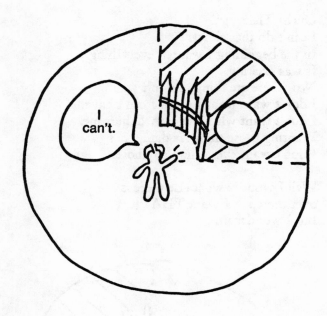

But look,
there are so many other interesting things.
Look at THAT! I want THAT!

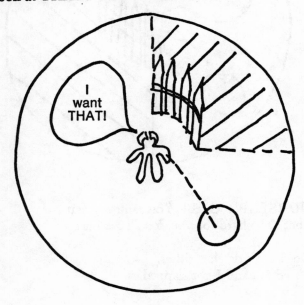

You: *NO.* (SLAP!)
Don't try that! You'll get hurt if you do.

me: Ouch! That hurt.
I can't do that either.
In the beginning I wanted everything.
It was exciting.
Now there are things I don't want.
I don't want what I think I can't have.
I don't want what I think will hurt me.
Wanting those things is dangerous.
I don't want everything anymore.

Well I wonder what else there is . . .
over there . . . I want THAT!
But I wonder if . . .

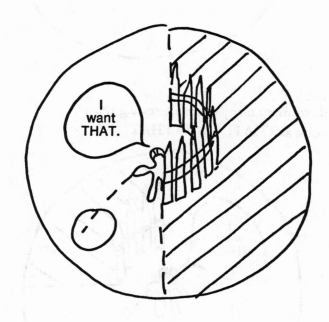

You: *NO.* (SLAP!) Ouch! You can't try that.
That's too hard for you. You'll get hurt.

me: Oh. I can't do that either.
I tried . . . and I got slapped.

That hurt. I don t like to hurt.
I'll stay away from that too.

You: That's good.

me: Gee . . . everything used to be so much fun.
Now there are things that hurt.
I don't want to do *everything* any more.
There are things I can't do now . . .

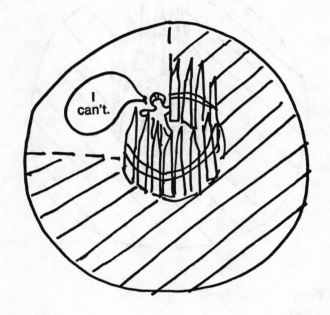

I'm getting fenced in,
and I really want THAT!
I'm going to try again.
Ouch! I fell, whah!
That really hurt.

You: I told you not to try that again.
You're bad. (SLAP!SLAP!)

me: Wow!

You: And DON'T FORGET!
I told you that before.

me: On second thought,
I don't want to do that.
I can't. It hurt. I don't like to hurt.
I'll stay out of there.

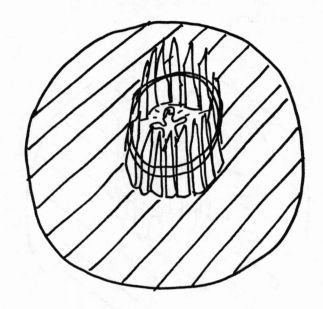

I've got the picture!
This is me.

This is the part of everything I CAN do,
that's OK for me, safe,
that you allow me to do.
This part of my system is **+** for me.

And this is MY DANGER ZONE.
This is the part of everything
that's not safe for me,
that I can't do.
I'm afraid of MY DANGER ZONE.

When I want things in there,
I get hurt.
Sometimes I get slapped; sometimes I fall,
I get scraped or cut.
I don't like to hurt.
I want to stay out of there.

I need you to do all those things I can't,
and I need you to tell me what is safe.
I can't make it without you, without what you do for me.
This part of everything is not mine.
This part is yours, you.
This part is (−) for me.

And this is my fence,
between what I can do
and MY DANGER ZONE.
Using your *NO*s and your SLAPS
and my falls and my hurts as a guide,
I put up my fence so as not to accidentally
get into DANGER.
I wonder if it is like this for others too?

Here's how my system works.
Whenever something new happens
I compare what I see and hear outside
with the images and soundtracks I have stored inside
about things that happened to me before.
I look and listen to the things that seem
to be similar or the same.
I compare them so I can decide*

* *Interesting word*, de cide. *Like* sui cide *and* homi cide, de cide *is to kill off
the alternative.*

what I can do and what I can't do now.
I compare the new things I am seeing and hearing
with the old ones I have seen.
And I give the new things meaning now
according to what I had decided about
what happened *before*,
according to whether what I'm comparing to
was stored in the part of my system that was SAFE
or whether it was stored as part of MY DANGER ZONE.
If what I say it is like was safe,
I feel it's safe, I feel I can.
If what I say it's like was dangerous,
I feel scared, I feel I can't.

The past is my reference.
It is important to remember about *then*
so I can know about *now*.

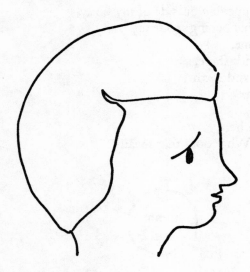

There are so many new things happening *outside* of me,
I need to know what I can and what I can't do.

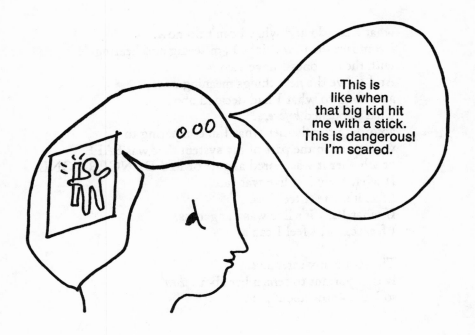

Besides the things happening outside of my body,
there are also things happening *inside* my body.
I sense things inside me,
a twitch here, a warmth there,
energy moving back and forth.
What does that mean?
I ask you.
I say, I have a twitch here
and a warmth there. What does that mean?

And you look into your system
about twitches here and warmths there,
and you give me a label
from your system to put on my sensation.

I need you to tell me whether that twitch
is safe or not,
whether I should like it or not.
You also tell me what that energy means
I should do.
When I have certain sensations in my stomach,
you say that means I am sick.
That is bad, that means I have to go to bed.

When I have certain sensations in my mouth,
you say that tastes good, umm.
But certain other sensations you say are bad.
You make me spit it out.
I don't like that.

I have certain sensations in my stomach and throat,
and you say I am scared,
that there is danger for me. Look out.
I don't like that.

Then certain other sensations in my stomach and throat
mean I am excited, eager.
Something good is happening.
I like that.

But it is difficult for me to figure out
which are which on my own.
When I ask you, you look inside of you,
and you ask yourself what that sensation means to you,
and then you tell me what it should mean to me.

I use you to help me decide which labels to use
for my sensations.
I let those sensations in my body mean to me
what you say the sensations you think are the same
mean to you.

It is like using your manual for 'how to be you'
to tell me 'how to be me.'

But gradually I forgot about having asked you
and what you replied.
I no longer notice my twitches
and warmths, my energies moving back and forth.
I notice only the meanings or labels
that I have learned from you.

I say to myself, that *feels* good,
that *feels* bad, that *feels* safe,
that *feels* dangerous,
so I can or so I can't do it.

How I *feel* tells me what to do or not to do.
It is comfortable, safe, knowing what to do.
I like being comfortable. I don't like to hurt.
My system for knowing what I can and what I can't,
what's safe and what's dangerous,
feels right to me.

They are my feelings, my sense-labels.
That is how it feels to be *me*.

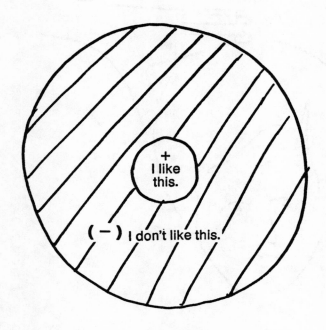

Things have been going along pretty smoothly—
my system works for me.
I don't get hurt so much any more.
I know me. I know about MY DANGER ZONE.
and I have my fence around me to protect me
from accidentally getting into DANGER.

Now you say I'm going to go to school.
I'll have friends. I'll do things on my own,
but you are afraid I'll forget.
You keep reminding me of the rules.

   "Never talk to strangers.
   Never cross the street alone.
   Always do what your teacher says.
   Never do dangerous things."

I know, Mom and Dad. I won't forget.
I know how to figure out what is safe for me.

You: We're proud of you.
You're such a GOOD CHILD!

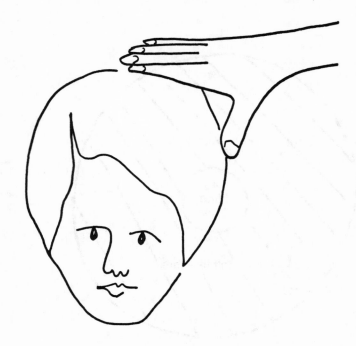

me: It's my first day of school.
Look, there are others out there
doing things that are different.
It sounds like fun!
I look closely.

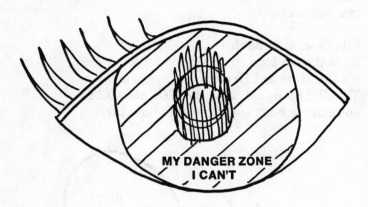

They're doing things I can't do,
things that are dangerous for me.
I feel scared. I want to go home.
That was the first time I really noticed.
I see everything new as in MY DANGER ZONE.
I look at life, everything new, through
my fence.

But Mom said always to do what my teacher says.
My teacher says it's OK, go ahead and play.
I can't just sit here safe and alone.
Here I go again.
Over there, what's THAT?
I want to do THAT!

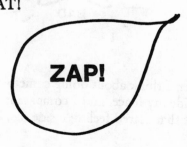

"DON'T DO THAT. THAT'S DANGEROUS.
YOU'LL GET HURT."

What was that?

I could hear Mom and Dad's voice.
And there was a jittery, twitchy sensation in my body
that felt dangerous.

I don't want to do that.
Even though I am all alone,
it's like Mom and Dad are here inside me.
The SLAPS from before, the *NO*s, the ouches
got into my body somehow, into how I feel.

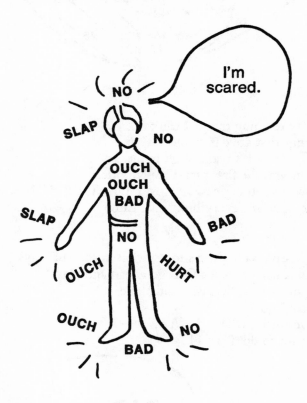

When I think about doing something
outside my fence, and I compare it to old scary pictures,
I get that scared feeling inside me. ZAP!

It's my body's signal to turn back
to the safe ways, the ways that worked before,
the ways I know I CAN.

There is a charge in my body
between I CAN and I CAN'T,
like Dad's battery
when he hooks the positive and the negative
poles together.

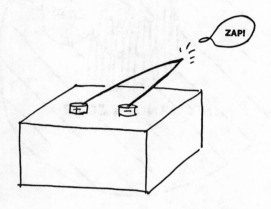

Ah, I know.
Whenever I try something new
I connect my +es and my −es together—
what I say I can and what I say I can't,
what I say I like and what I say I don't.

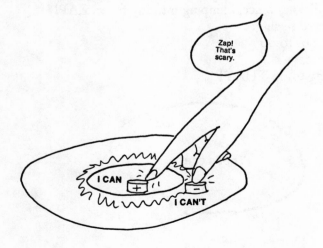

No wonder there's a Zap.
There's electricity in my fence!

I have an electric fence,
like a cow in a pasture. ZAP!
That feeling fence reminds me to
stay out of DANGER.
But my teacher is still waiting.
She's looking at me.
I don't like my fence, bumping into my fence. ZAP!
This scared feeling. . .
but I've got to do
what she says.
I'm going to do THAT!

I did it.

You know, that wasn't so bad.

Look what I got!

What I can do has been expanded.

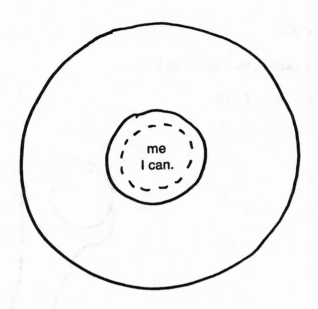

I *can* do lots of new things:
running, jumping, spelling, headstands, flips.
But now that I have learned your rules,
you are telling me to do things
you had told me *never* to do,
like "never cross the street alone"
and "never talk to strangers."
I look at the street, and then I look and listen inside,
and it feels bad, dangerous. I'm scared of the street.
Now you tell me to ask strangers things if I don't know.
When I look inside, I'm scared of strangers.
I still hear all those old warnings
I stored inside me from before.
Now my teacher wants me to be in a play.
I'll have to be up in front of
strangers.

The things that were true before aren't true now.
Everything's changing.

I can do those things, *but it doesn't feel right.*
I feel afraid. ZAP!

My feeling fence is still in the same old place.
I need to put some gates in my feeling fence
so I can go out to explore a little
and still have my fence there in case I need it.
I want to see if I can move my fence out now
so I can feel able to do some of the things
that used to be dangerous for me with my small body.

But there's the ZAP.

Those scared feelings keep me from accidentally
doing dangerous things.
But they also keep me from doing NEW THINGS,
things I couldn't do before with my little body,
things that used to be too hard.

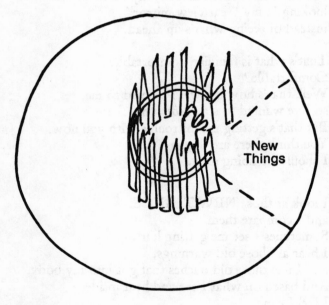

Things are changing.
My body is growing.

And as I can do much more,
I have to expand my fence too.
There are more and more things that I can do now.
But they still don't look right inside to me,
    they still don't sound right inside to me,
    they still don't feel right inside to me,
when I compare them with before.
I'm not sure about me, about my system now.
I need to take a closer look.

How do I get past my feeling fence, the ZAP,
those scared feelings?
I'm used to how my system works.
I'm used to looking back at what I don't want
rather than ahead to what I do want.
I seem to have spent most of my time
looking in my "rear view mirror"
instead of seeing what's up ahead.

That's what is familiar, comfortable.
Comfortable?
Well, that's how it always seemed to me,
so I've wanted to stay *behind* my fence.
But that's getting me in trouble with you now.
You think there are things
I should be doing now.

I look at those NEW THINGS,
and I compare them.
Sometimes I see me getting hurt.
I hear all those old warnings,
and I feel those old ouches that got into my body.
And based on what I see and hear inside,
I feel I can't,
so I don't.

Sometimes I see I've done that before,
so I tell myself I can.

It feels OK then.
Then I really can do it.

Sometimes I see I can't, and I won't.
I hear myself saying, I can't, I can't,
I'll get hurt.
I imagine myself bumping into my fence. ZAP!

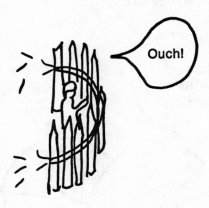

I like it when you are around me.
Then, when I'm not sure, I can ask you.

And you say "You *can* do that.
TRUST ME. I KNOW YOU are able to do that now.
You're old enough, you're big enough."
You go inside and you see me doing it.

You look and you tell me how.
Then I can see me doing it too.
You say I can do it,
so I say I can do it too.
Then it feels right to me,
and I can do it.

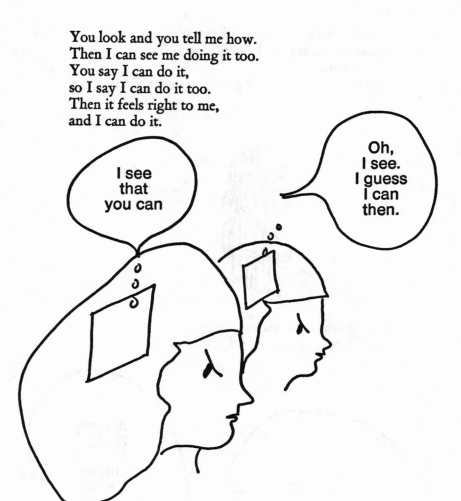

And most of the time you do know.
I've learned to trust you.
But now I'm not sure about me any more.
I can't trust me, my old system,
the old pictures I use as a reference,
the old familiar soundtracks I listen to,
my old feelings.

Things keep changing.
I keep growing and doing new things.
I want to ask you about more and more new things.
Mommy, Daddy, do you think I can?

But there is a price for your advice.
Sometimes when I ask you about what I want,
you get upset.
You say,

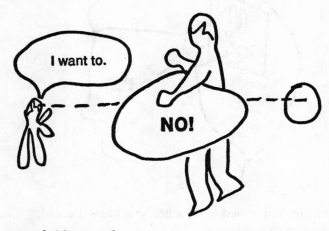

NO.
YOU CAN'T DO THAT.
IF YOU DO, I'LL PUNISH YOU!

Now you are preventing me from doing what I want,
from doing things I see I can do,
things I've told myself I can do
that feel OK to me now.

I want to.

NO!

I don't like you then.
You don't feel like a part of me,
of my system.

I learned to do what my friends could do.
They were doing things you said never to do.
I was scared at first, but
I would watch what they did
till I could see me doing it,

till I said to myself I could do that too,
till I felt I could, and then
I'd do it.

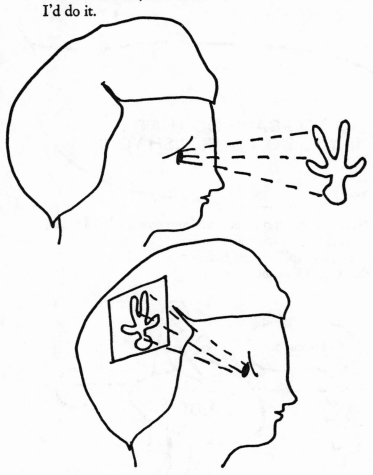

It's not like it used to be when you knew I could,
and you cheered me on.

Now as I expanded me, as I could do more
and more things,
it was getting harder and harder for me to be with you.
I began to have secrets from you.
I figured what you didn't know
wouldn't hurt me or
my chances of getting what I needed from you.

But then I felt separate.
That secret was between us.
It kept us apart.*

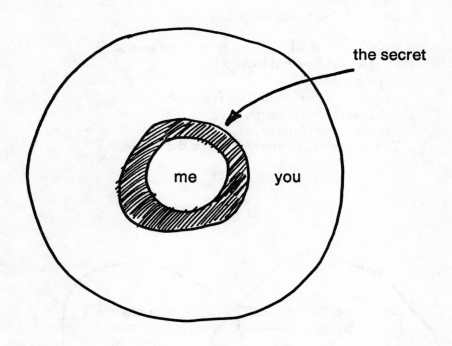

the secret

me   you

We can't really be together now.
I don't like that.
I want you to still be a part of me,
to continue doing what I need.

* *Interesting word*, a part.

I'll experiment to see how different
you will allow me to be,
and still do for me what I need from you.

But sometimes you don't give me dinner,
or you won't let me go outside and play.
I need those things from you.
I'm afraid to even ask you now.
I see how upset you got before.
I hear that *NO*, and "if you do then you won't
be able to. . . ."
I don't even like to imagine myself asking you now.
I tell myself *NO*.
So now I don't even ask you anymore.

I try to look at what I want from in my system
to figure out how it'd look to you
in your system.
I try to do things I think are OK with you.
But I don't always know.
Sometimes you surprise me.
You do things differently than you did before.

I always thought you could do everything
that I couldn't do.

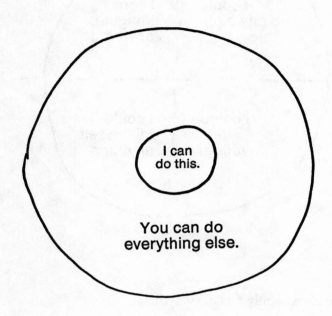

I can
do this.

You can do
everything else.

But now I know that
there are things that *you can't do* too.

I remember when it all began.

I was all there is, everything.

I could imagine anything I wanted.

I could think or say to myself anything I wanted.

I could feel anything.

I could do anything.

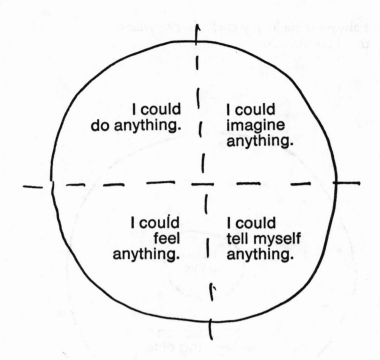

Doing was only *part* of everything,
until
I discovered my small body and your body.
I compared me with you
from the *outside*.

I didn't notice that I could still
safely do anything I wanted *inside*.

I could imagine, think, feel, or sense
anything, everything.

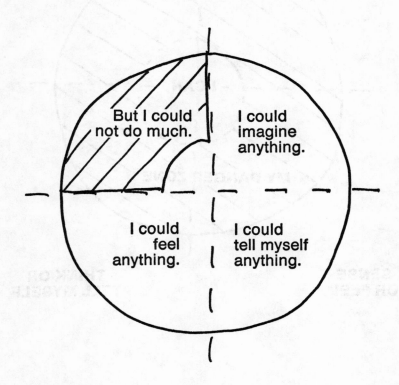

I decided* that if I couldn't *do* as much as you,
then I couldn't *be* as much as you.

I decided that I shouldn't imagine what I shouldn't do.
I shouldn't talk about what I shouldn't do either.
I shouldn't feel anything I shouldn't do.

* *Remember about* de-cide.

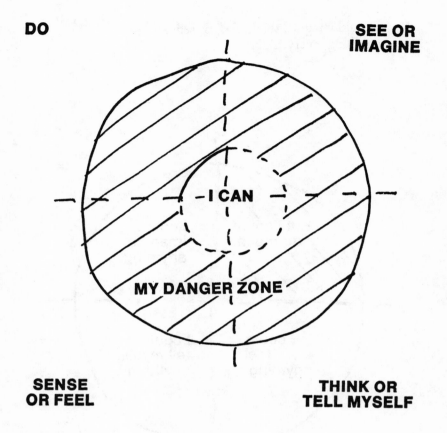

DO

SEE OR IMAGINE

I CAN

MY DANGER ZONE

SENSE OR FEEL

THINK OR TELL MYSELF

That's how I decided on where my fence
should go,
what I can and can't imagine, say,
feel, or do.

So when I built my fence to protect my little body
from what I couldn't safely do,
I made it go all around me.

DO

**SEE OR
IMAGINE**

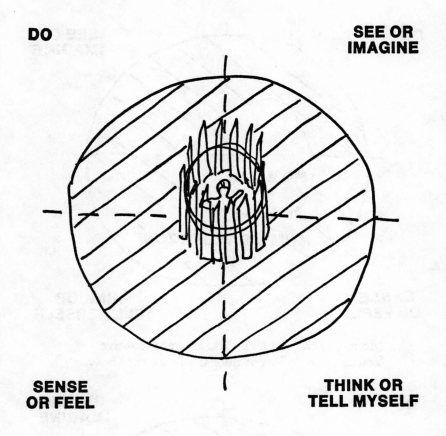

**SENSE
OR FEEL**

**THINK OR
TELL MYSELF**

I limited myself in all the other parts of WHO I AM.
I limited what I could imagine or see inside.
I limited what I could tell myself inside,
what I could think.
I limited what I thought was safe to feel inside,
so I'd be safe.

I see now that my system
for what's safe and what's dangerous
is different from yours.

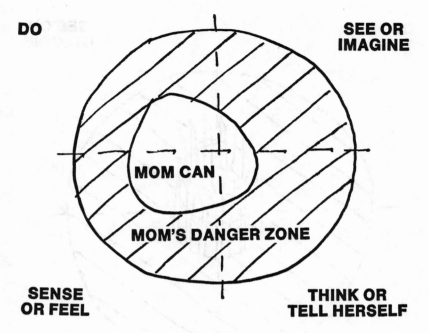

Mom, you can feel a lot. You are very sensitive.
You can also do lots of things; you are very busy.

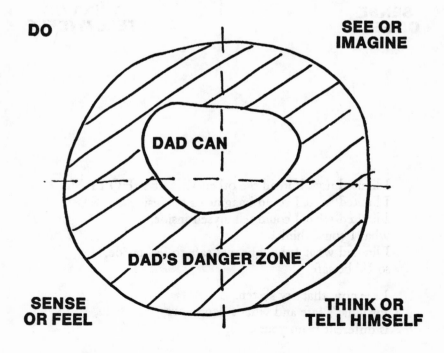

Dad's system is different.
Dad, you can imagine other things.
You see and plan in your mind, and then
you can do whatever it takes to make
things happen.

I'm more of a dreamer, a thinker.

DO

**SEE OR
IMAGINE**

I CAN

MY DANGER ZONE

**SENSE
OR FEEL**

**THINK OR
TELL MYSELF**

Our systems each look different. We are different.
That's very useful and fun, except
when I try to make you be like me,
or you try to make me be like you.

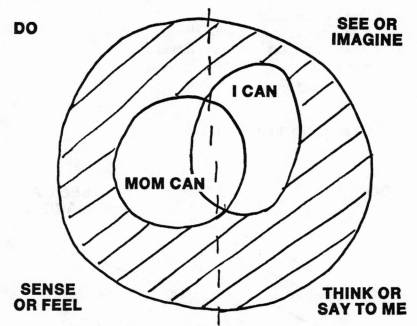

DO

SEE OR
IMAGINE

I CAN

MOM CAN

SENSE
OR FEEL

THINK OR
SAY TO ME

For Mom, my system is pretty scary.
A lot of me is now in her DANGER ZONE.
For her, that part of me is wrong.

A lot of what I can do is in Dad's DANGER ZONE too.

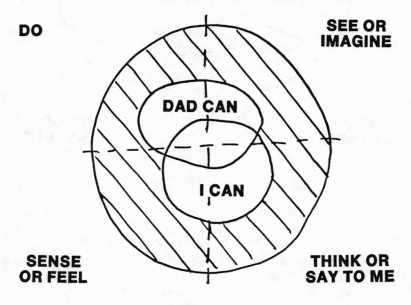

DO

SEE OR
IMAGINE

DAD CAN

I CAN

SENSE
OR FEEL

THINK OR
SAY TO ME

Sometimes Mom says that what I want is OK,
but Dad says NO.

Sometimes Dad says what I want is OK,
but Mom says NO.
It's sure confusing when they don't agree.
I wonder sometimes if they really love *me*.
They try to make me do things *their way*,
I don't know what that means, *their way*,
where they really agree
or where they back each other up.

I guess I'll just have to pick the parts
of their systems that I want.
I'd like to please Mom and Dad,
but I guess I can only please *me*.

If I'm home on time,
    my room is neat,
    my grades are OK,
we seem to get along pretty well.

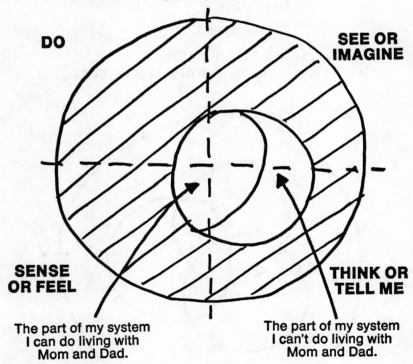

DO

SEE OR IMAGINE

SENSE OR FEEL

THINK OR TELL ME

The part of my system
I can do living with
Mom and Dad.

The part of my system
I can't do living with
Mom and Dad.

Once I got home very late.
My mother was worried.
My father was furious.

NO. (SLAP!)

I didn't get to go out for two weeks.
That hurt!
I'd better watch their rules.
I really was in their DANGER ZONES.
It's hard to talk to them.
They get upset when I ask about things
I want to know.
They say it's not nice to talk
about things like that!
Sometimes they yell, or they get all red,
or I get sent to my room.
In their systems, they can't talk about those things.
They are dangerous for them.
So they think they are dangerous for me too.
That's what they know when they make
their internal comparisons.
It's hard for me to tell them
the truth for me.

I guess there's no THE TRUTH,
but just how it looks to each of us in our systems.

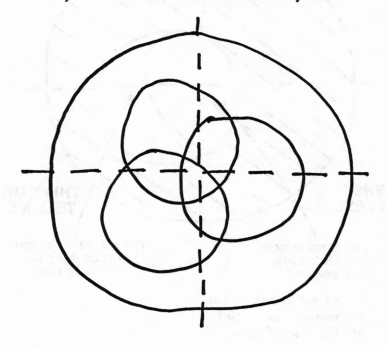

2

To others:
How much I needed you

me: I am meeting more and more of you.
I see you are *all* different.
It's not just me and you.

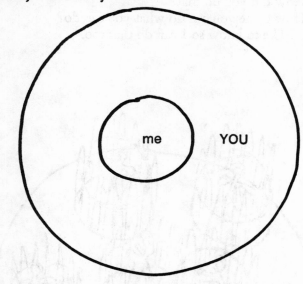

It's me and *all of you*.

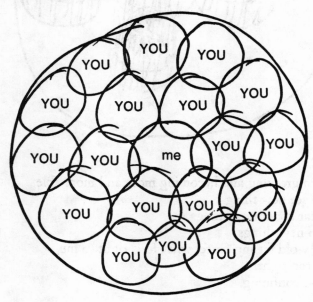

You all have your systems, your own fences.
But all of your fences are in different places.
You imagine things differently, think,
feel, and do things differently.
That's exciting!
How did you do that?
How come you can do what you can do?
I'd like to know so I can do that too.

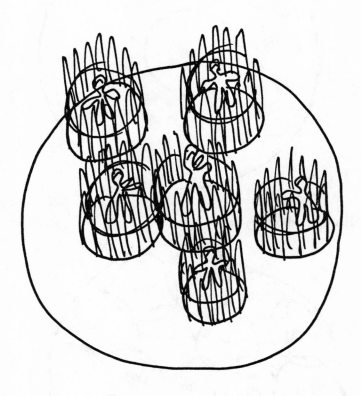

I'm growing and becoming more and more able
to see new things,
hear about new things,
do new things.
My old feeling fence, what feels right to me,
is too tight,
too confining.

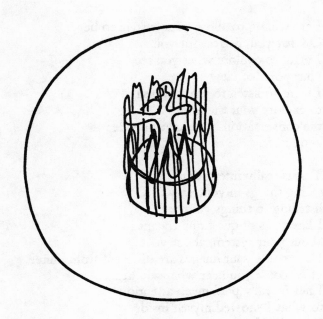

I am opening up my gate
and moving out into one of your systems.
I want to explore your system,
how your system works.

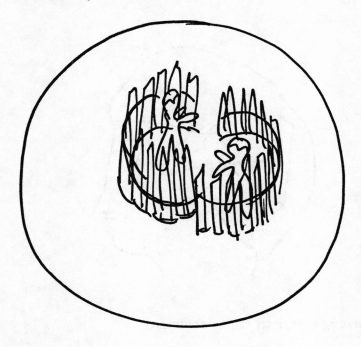

I am willing to allow your system to be
OK for you, perfect for you.
I want to explore what you see,
your point of view.
I want to listen to what you say,
to explore your thoughts,
the conversations you have outside
and inside.

This is really interesting*,
seeing things in your way,
listening to things your way.
I have lots of questions I want to ask
about your system, about you.
How come your images are different from mine?
How come you hear what you hear?
I never really paid much attention
to what I showed myself inside.
How did those movies get there?
I guess I've just shown myself things
automatically so far.

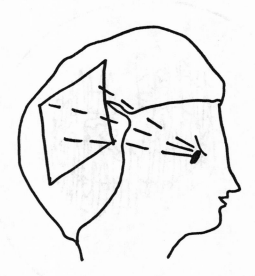

* *Interesting word*, inter est, *to be within.*

I am trying on your system.
I am seeing how it would be for me
imagining things your way.
I am talking to me about your thoughts,
feeling about your ways.
I am beginning to include parts of you, your system,
in my expanded system for how to be me.

As I try on your system,
I am recording in me new pictures,
new soundtracks
that I can use for future comparisons
that I'll make inside.
So I can see me doing what you do.

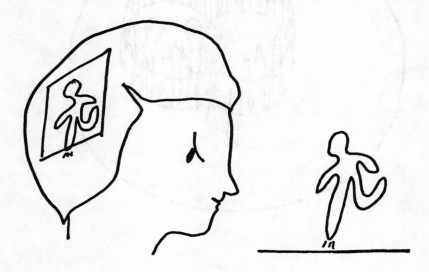

Seeing those new films
of what I can do
allows me to feel differently,
allows me to move my feeling fence
out into new territory.
I am learning to move into your system,
to take your point of view to discover more of me.
I couldn't understand you
when I looked from within my system into yours.
You never made sense to me from over here.

Now I see how you see things.
Now I am hearing your thinking.
It's different when I come from where you are.
I understand you now.
I understand more about me too.

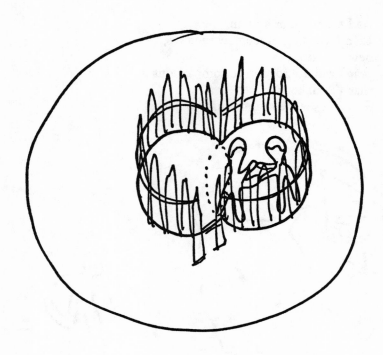

I am enjoying being in your system,
until I switch,
until I go back into my system and look
at your system through my system.
Then I feel scared.
Then what you are doing is dangerous for me.
Your way is wrong, bad, dangerous.
Then I feel you shouldn't do that either.
That's wrong for me, and it's wrong for you.
Then I feel I need to control you
so I can be comfortable being with you.

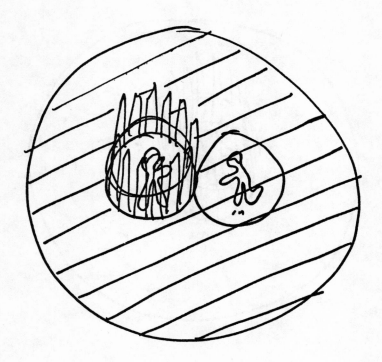

But I don't think about it being my fence then,
the one I built for me,
the limits I've chosen for me.

I blame you. I think you are wrong.
I want to avoid you.
I don't even notice that the discomfort
is inside of me.

What you are doing is comfortable for you.
It's the way you usually do things.
I am the one creating the discomfort within me.

My comfort is more important to me then
than my exploring.

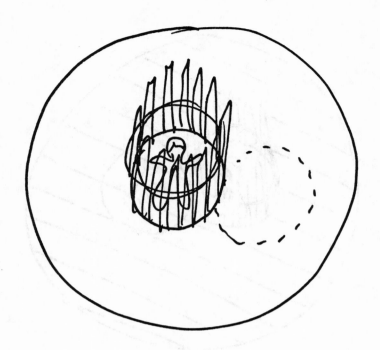

As long as I allow you to be you,
as long as I allow you to have your own system,
you are open to me.
You let me explore what you see,
your thoughts, your feelings, your ways.
I can try on your system and
begin to see me that way, think about me that way,
and feel and do things that way too.
I can include the experiences of me
I am having through you
in my experience.
Being in your system,
I can record in me new images, new dialogues.
Those new images and dialogues become
a part of my internal system,
ready to use the next time I see new things,
the next time I have to decide whether
I can do something or not.

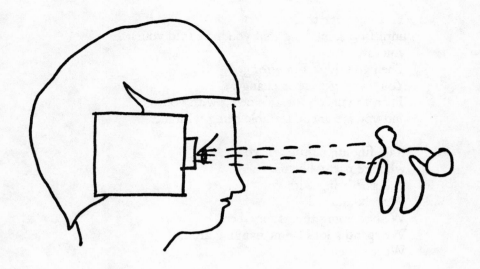

When I'm interested in you,
you are interested in my system too.
You are asking lots of question about my system.
You are expanding your system too.
It is fun sharing.
There are parts of our systems that are alike,
things we have in common.

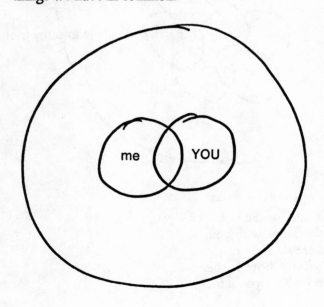

You enjoy me too,
until I do something that you have told yourself
you can't do.
Then you think I'm wrong.
You try to get me to change.
Then I'm uncomfortable being with you,
and you are uncomfortable being with me.

I am finding a group of you
who are partly like me.
It is safe being with you.
We talk and talk.
We like doing things together.
We spend a lot of time hanging around.
We are friends.

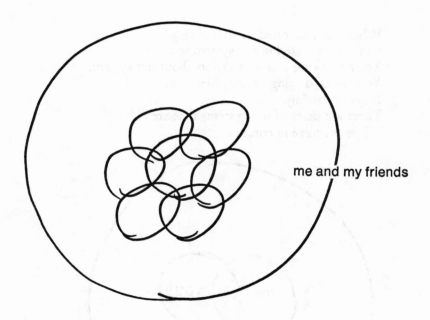

me and my friends

It is safe for me to be with you,
to do things with you.
We are a lot alike.
You know how I'll be,
I know how you'll be.

We have a territory that is agreed upon,
understood,
the way we are together.
I am expanding my fence with you around.
I can see, say, feel and do new things
with you around.

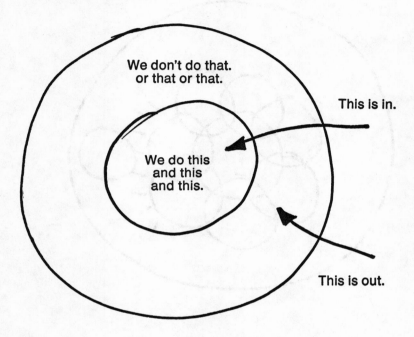

We don't do that.
or that or that.

This is in.

We do this
and this
and this.

This is out.

We have
　our *in* jokes,
　our *in* clothes,
　our *in* words,
　our *in* ways.
We all protect each other
from other people we don't like,
who aren't like us,
who don't do things the way we do.
My friends are a part of me now.
My friends are like my fence,
keeping me away from others who are dangerous.
I need you to do the things I want to do,
to go out with, to hang around with.

With you I feel included. I am "in."
I am agreed with.
Everything feels OK.

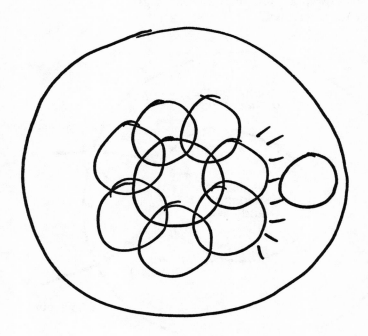

I have grown a lot hanging around with you.
Things are beginning to tighten around me.
Now you are telling me that
there are things I have to do to be with you.
"You have to do this, you shouldn't say that,
or wear this."
There are rules for being in the group.
I've met someone new,
and I'm interested in exploring that new system,
but my friends are here now.
I feel pressure.
I still want them to like me, to include me,
but they don't like this new person
that I am interested in.

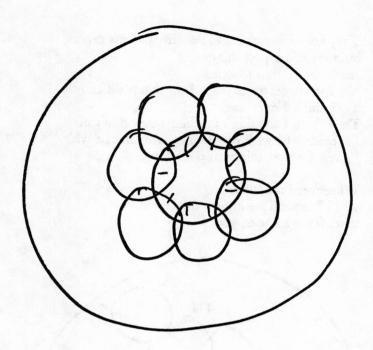

They say, "We don't like
    the way he does things,
    the way he dresses,
    how he talks,
    who he hangs out with."*
They don't like his system.

They don't even know his system.
I have explored him a little.
I can see a lot of things his way.
Things look different his way.
It is exciting.
I like him, and he likes me too.
He feels OK to me.

It is beginning to sound very familiar.
Like Mom and Dad, my friends think
there are certain things I should do,
certain ways I should think and feel.

* *Language is interesting*—"things got all bent out of shape," "it blew
them away," "when push comes to shove."

They are different things than my parents expect,
but they still expect things
according to *their* systems.
My friends get upset when I do things differently.
They think I'm wrong.
They think I shouldn't do things they don't do.
I shouldn't be with people they wouldn't be with.
I guess I expect things of them too.

Whenever I am different,
when I expand me in new directions,
that affects some of you.

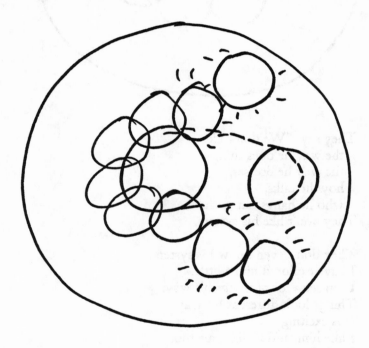

I am exploring to see how different
you will let me be and still hang around with me.
I need you.
I am figuring out my system now for how I have to be
to be OK with you.
I just want to explore,
to begin expanding my system
to my full potential,

but I still know there are some things I can't do
and still be your friend.
I have you around me reminding me,
"That's not like you. You never were like that before.
We're disappointed. You've changed.
You are not like you used to be."
You don't want me to change,
to expand my territory,
to try out others' ways, others' ideas.
That's scary for you, uncomfortable.
You're afraid I'll change.
Then maybe we wouldn't be alike,
maybe we wouldn't be friends any more.

Now, even though I could be with lots more of you,
I hang around only with you.
Expanding me is scary for me too, uncomfortable.
I'm afraid I'll change or you'll change,
and we won't be friends any more.
I don't want to run the risk of being
all alone.

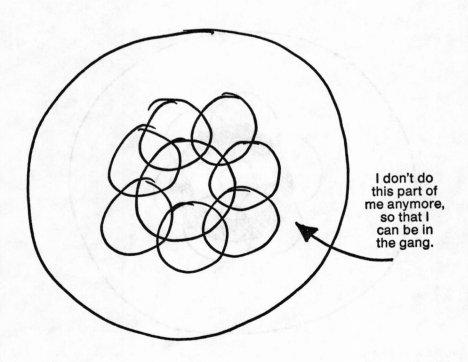

I don't do
this part of
me anymore,
so that I
can be in
the gang.

I am feeling a little trapped.
I know there is more for me out there,
but it is risky exploring with my friends around.
I don't like to upset you.
I want to keep you liking me,
and I want to do what I want.

I am beginning to have secrets from you.
Those secrets are between us.
I don't like that.
I want to tell someone about what I'm discovering,
but I'm afraid it'll get around
and I'll be out.
So I can't tell any of you.
It is safe and familiar having my friends,
but I feel confined, separate.
You are around me,
but not a part of me,
not really interested in me
or me in you.

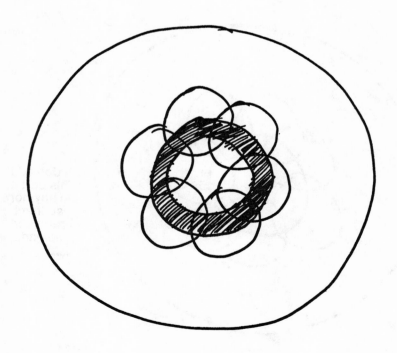

High school and living at home
are nearly over.
I am going away to college,
moving away on my own,
away from home,
from my parents whose systems I know,
from my friends whose systems I know.
I am a little uncomfortable.
Everything is unfamiliar.
Who am I?
What do I want?
It's more than uncomfortable.
I'm scared.

I have to decide what to do with my life,
how to take care of me.
There are things I haven't done for me yet,
the things you have always done for me.
I never really noticed how
letting you take care of me
allows me *not* to take care of me,
how when I make you response-able for me,
I give up being response-able for me.
I see that I have relied on your doing
instead of expanding me into your system
and trying on your knowing of how to do
what you do for me.
I have wanted you to do it for me.
I haven't cared much about my learning to do for me,
so now I can't. I don't know how.
And you aren't here.
I'm all alone and unable,
and I want to blame you for what I don't do,
for what I don't get.

What do I want to do in my life?
That is the question my parents are asking me,
that is the question my friends are asking me,
that is the question I am asking me.
What do I want to do with my life?
But I don't know.

I keep looking for someone who'll tell me.
That's how it has always worked before.
Someone else knew,
and they'd tell me what was best for me.
But now everyone is asking me,
and I don't know.

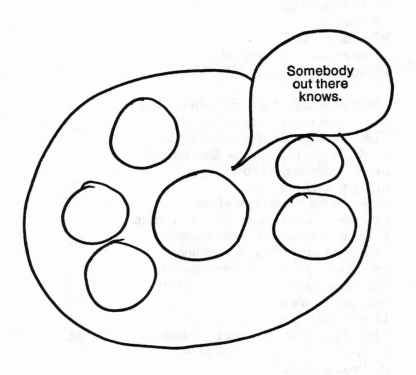

I know how it has been.
I have referred to my old pictures,
my old soundtracks, to figure out how.
Then my old feelings come up,
and as long as I stay in my fence,
things feel familiar.
I know how to figure out what to do.
But I don't know much about creating my future,
about what is up ahead.

I am still afraid of what I don't know,
of new things, of other ways,
of you, of your systems,
of being response-able for me,
of choosing for me.

I have to make my own decisions now,
what to major in,
what career do I want to pursue,
who will I marry,
how do I have to be so somebody'll love me,
want me?
It is scary, and I am alone.
I don't have my friends around me either.
I don't really feel like me without
my friends around.
I want to find new friends.
But it's different now.
Nobody here knows me,
knows how I was as a kid growing up at home,
knows how I was in school,
knows the friends I hung out with.
They don't know about my successes and failures,
my reputation.

They don't know my history.

I got spanked for.
I was scared when. It hurt.
I always do. I never can. Mom says
I should. Dad really likes. Good children
always. It's nice to. It's polite to.
I can try to. It's dangerous to think.
I would never go. It's unimagineable that I.
Dad gets upset when I. Mom prefers that I.
To get along at home I must. Never forget
to. I have to be careful to. I don't
want to hurt. I'm not good at.
I'll probably fail at.
Doing that is risky.

I can be different.
I can be any way I want.
I can see me any way I want,
tell myself anything I want,
tell you anything I want,
I can feel and do anything I want.

Nobody knows me here
but me.

But I want them to know me, the old me.
So I tell them all about me,
about my old system.
Now they know me. They know my history,
what I have and haven't done,
how I was and how I wasn't,
how I've always been,
what I liked and what I didn't,
how I felt about things.

Now you know about my fence too.
I've taught you to see me the way I see me,
so you don't ask me to do things I haven't done.
You don't think about me any way you want.
You think about me the way I've told you,
the way I've been.

I'm comfortable with my limits.
As long as you allow my limits too,
I'm comfortable with you.

I am less scared now.
I have made new friends.
I can make more new friends, too.
I still want you to like me,
to agree with me,
but I am more on my own.
I don't need to be with any one of you.
I can take care of me.

I am beginning to see that I can choose
who I want to be with and who I don't,
who is fun for me to do things with.
I like to do things that you like too.

It is interesting for me to watch me making friends.
I try to find out how you are like me,
what we have in common.

That way I can decide whether I like you,
whether I want to spend time with you,
whether I think we will get along.

I like the ways we are alike.
I spend a lot of time seeing the alike parts,
but it takes me quite a while
before I get around to exploring the ways
we are different.

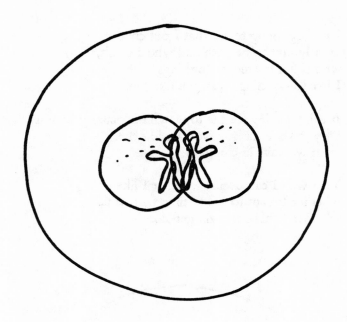

When I begin to look at the ways we aren't alike,
sometimes I feel I don't like you.
Sometimes I have doubts about you.
You scare me. Well, that is,
your system scares me.
Your different images that you see and share with me
scare me, your different thoughts,
the things that you say.
I judge you.
I say your system is wrong, wrong for you,
instead of seeing
it's wrong for me, given the limits
I have put on me, given my fence.
Your system is perfect for you,
and your system is a potential part of me,
the expanding me.

When I spend time looking at how we're different
and how dangerous your ways are,
I feel I have to protect me from you.

I don't like you, your system.
Those pictures, those soundtracks, scare me.
So I put up my fence.
I feel separate.

I don't feel as comfortable about the parts
of your system that are different.
That's interesting, isn't it?
Where your system is different from mine,
where I can explore *new* things with you,
try on different ways,
that is the part that I don't like,
that is uncomfortable.
I prefer you to be like me.
I prefer me to be like me, the old me.
I prefer to have your agreement to my limits
rather than your point of view on my expansion.

I know how to keep me safe,
to keep things the same
by constantly comparing everything new
to my recordings of the past.
That way when I see it's like something old,
when I tell myself it's like something old,
I feel I know what to do.
I do what I did before. That feels safe.
But I want to discover new ways.
I want to expand me now.

When I use my old comparisons
I see you as able to do what I can't.
I tell myself what I've said before:
that I can't but you can,
so I feel I need you.
I need you to like me so I'll like me.
I need you to do what I can't do.
I feel I have to please you
so you will do what I need,
so you'll like me,
so you won't leave me.

But I know now that's no longer true.
I am as able as you,
but my system is different,
where I've placed my fence,
what I see and say inside.
In some areas I can do more, in some areas less.
My system works perfectly,
but how am I using it?
I can do anything I can think about.
I create my own feelings about my abilities
by the pictures I show myself inside,
by the dialogues I play inside my head.

If I keep looking at outdated movies,
I'll keep creating outdated feelings.

As long as I am seeing pictures of me as a child,
when I was not able to do everything,
when I really couldn't do much,
I'll feel I'm not able to do much.

Times have changed.
My body has grown. I am able.
But I'm still comparing me
with those childhood memories
and telling me I still can't
when I really can.
I must update my own internal pictures
and soundtracks,
and begin to make updated comparisons
so I'll feel ready to do what I am able to do.

I know now that all of your systems
are the rest of my system.
All of your ways are other ways
I could see things, say, feel,
or do things.
You, your systems, are very important parts
of my system.

Your ways are all the ways I might be.
Now I see why I need to explore you.

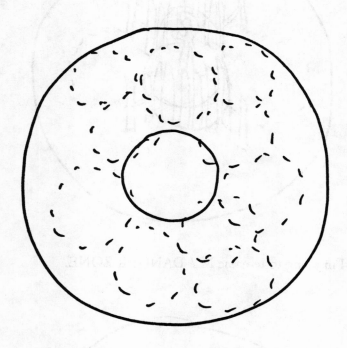

As I learn more about you, all of you,
I learn more about me.

I am beginning to put more and more gates
into my fence.
I want to be able to get out to explore
the rest of everything,
to try on some of your ways,
other ways I might be.

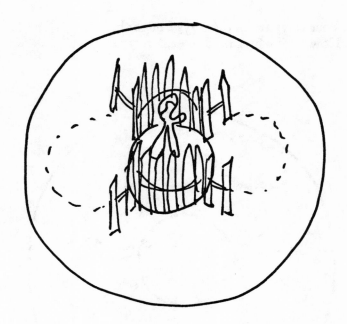

I'm going to re-name MY DANGER ZONE.

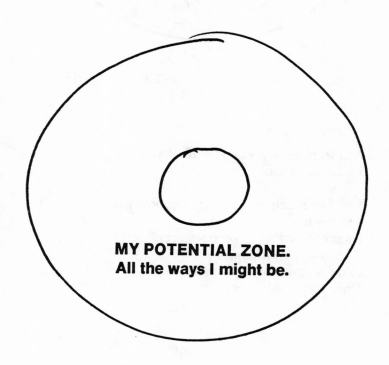

MY POTENTIAL ZONE.
All the ways I might be.

That seems to work a lot better for me.

But how do I get past my scared feelings?
Past the ZAP?
I can use the ZAP in my fence
to help me explore.
I can use that electricity
so I can see better what I'm doing.
What I need is a switch.
Then I could run that electricity
through my switch into a light
so I can see.

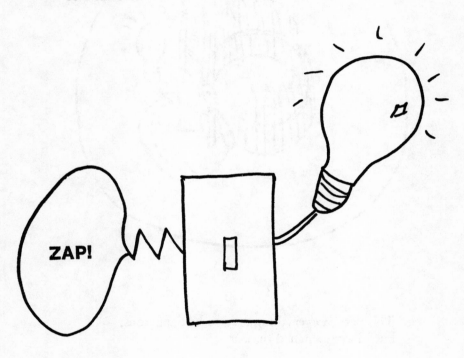

Then when I feel that ZAP,
I'll switch inside so I can see that
I am going through my gate
into one of your systems, into MY POTENTIAL ZONE,

into things that I'm not comfortable with yet,
things I don't allow me to do now,
into something new for me
and old for you.

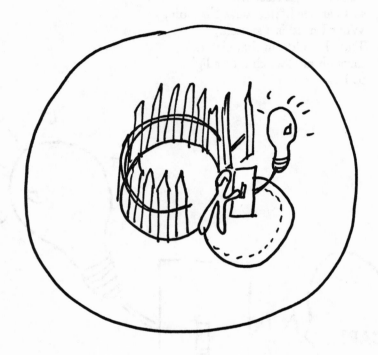

This part of everything used to be dangerous,
but I have switched that.

This might be something I CAN DO now,
something I want TO DO now,
that I just DON'T DO
because of my fence, my fear.

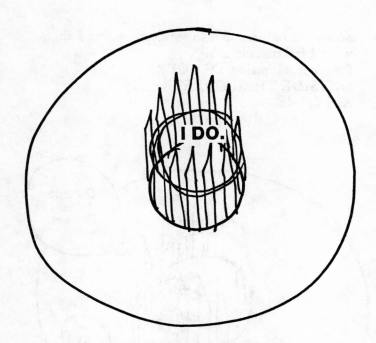

**I CAN, BUT I DON'T.
MY POTENTIAL ZONE.
All the things I might
be able to do.**

It's still scary for me exploring you,
your ways.
And sometimes when I get into your territory
I feel that ZAP,
And I forget that I am exploring.
I forget to switch.

So instead of being able to see clearly where I am,
when I feel that old ZAP
I think it is signaling DANGER,
OUTSIDE THREAT, RETREAT.
And so I do.

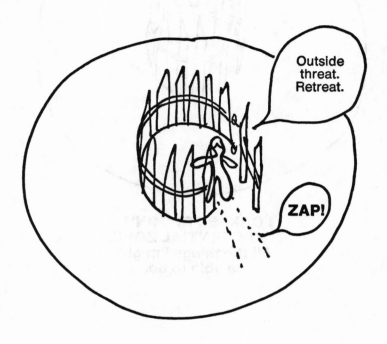

And then I think you caused my scare,
my unfamiliarity; or I get nervous,
and maybe I even fall.
And I yell at you,
"You hurt me, you upset me,
you scared me, and you made me fall,"
instead of remembering that
I was trying on an unfamiliar system,
ways that work for you
but are unfamiliar, uncomfortable for me now.

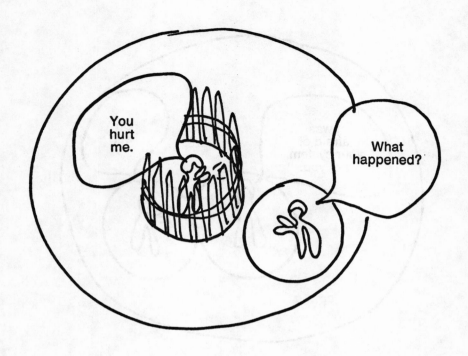

Now I remember.

So I switch, and I see
it's not you.
It's your system that I'm afraid of,
the ways you see things,
you think, and feel, and do things.
Those ways have been dangerous for me.

Now I tell you the truth.
It wasn't you. It was me,
my feeling fence, my ZAP.

I was not really afraid of you.

I was afraid of expanding me.

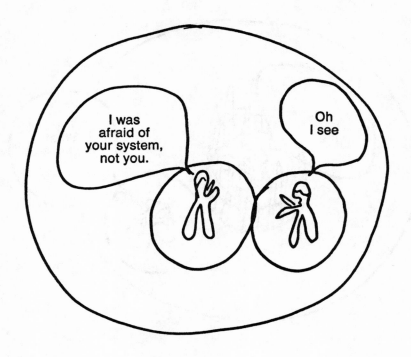

But if this time too I forget to switch
and I blame you
and I separate me from you,
I make my old system right again.
I prove it by telling myself,
"I was interested in you, and you hurt me.
I'll never do that again.
I'll never trust you."

Then I need my fence to protect me.
I tell myself, I'm good ++,
you're bad −−.
So I increase the charge.
I add more electricity to my fence.

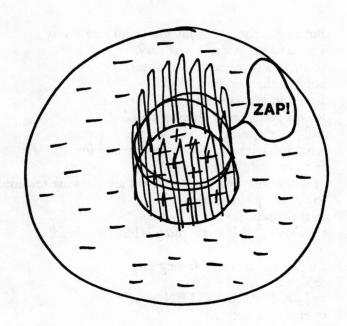

And with more charge
I now need more insulation,
so I stay away from you.
We don't talk.
I am separate.
I don't explore that part of MY POTENTIAL ZONE.
I avoid you, your system.

But there is another way I can use that electricity.
I am going to use that scary feeling, that ZAP,
as a signal to LOOK AND LISTEN
when I am crossing over into your system,
rather than automatically getting frightened
and turning back to my familiar old ways.
Like crossing a street,
just because I'm scared
doesn't mean I shouldn't ever cross.
I want to get over there now
to explore the rest of my system,
to explore your systems.

But to do that, to use my system in a new way,
I need to see you in a new way,
to see you as an expansion of me,
not as a threat to me.
I need to learn to distinguish between
what's going on in *my outer world*
and what's going on on my inner screen,
what I'm telling my body to be ready for.
Is there really danger now,
or is my body reacting to what I am showing me inside,
to my scary old pictures,
to the comparisons I'm making,
to what I say this new thing is like from before?

I will use that scared feeling now
to signal me, to be alert,
to LOOK AND LISTEN outside,
to explore whether
I'm on the brink of disaster according to my old view,
or I'm on the brink of discovery
according to my new view.

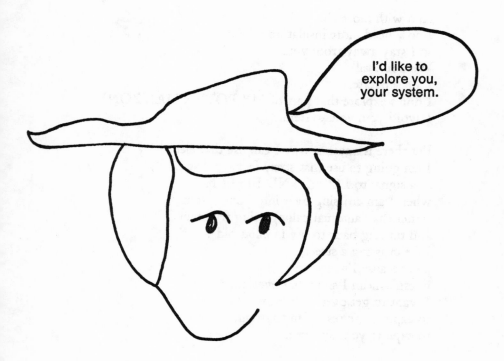

I'd like to
explore you,
your system.

I'm going to play life a whole new way.
I have a choice now.
I can play *a game of expanding me*, my system,
becoming more of everything, of me and you,
or
I can play *a game of protecting me* from you,
of defending my old fences,
trying to stay the same.

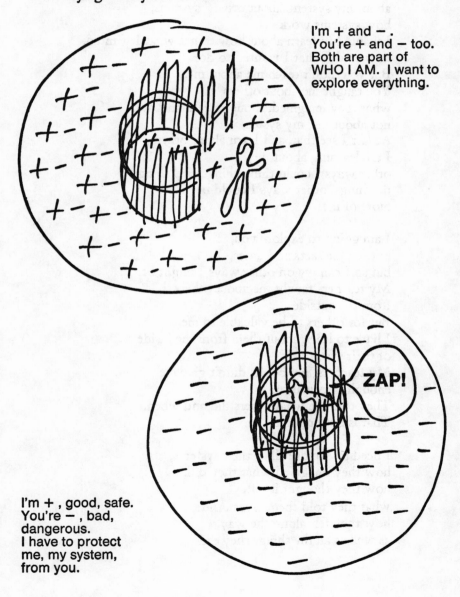

I'm + and − .
You're + and − too.
Both are part of
WHO I AM. I want to
explore everything.

ZAP!

I'm + , good, safe.
You're − , bad,
dangerous.
I have to protect
me, my system,
from you.

Everything I've ever done worked perfectly
to get me here.
Now, where do I want to go
and what new ways do I need to know
to get there?

I was excited going off to school.
I thought you would teach me all about me,
about my system, about others' systems,
how systems work.
I wanted to learn about how to get what I wanted,
how to do what I wanted to do.
But you didn't teach me about me.
You taught me about others,
what they imagined, thought, felt, and did,
not about me, my system.
At last I see that, as I learn about others,
I am learning about me,
other ways I could think things, feel things,
do things, other ways I could be
more of me.

I am going to explore you,
not for the facts and dates,
but so I can try on other ways I might be.
My teachers taught me about others
from the outside.
But for others to be valuable to me,
I have to learn about them from the inside
of their system.
My teachers, my books didn't give me
enough information.
They told me what others did and when.
That is not enough.

I need to explore all of their systems,
how they imagined what they did,
how they thought it out,
what they told themselves inside,
how they felt along the way,
as well as all the things they did.

I know now that
doing is only part of WHO I AM, of my system.
I am all that I imagine,
I am all that I say,
I am all that I feel or sense,
as well as all that I do.
I am really going to meet the people
I want to learn about.
Then I can explore their systems from the inside.
Then I will open up my gate and go inside.
I'm going to explore those of you
who can do what I want to do
so I can try on your systems.
I see that I CAN IF YOU CAN,
that WHAT I DON'T DO is WHAT I MIGHT DO.
I just have to re-position my fence pieces
so I can
> imagine it that way,
> think it that way,
> feel it that way,
> do it that way.

I understand about my feeling fence now.
It is useful protection when there is danger,
and it doesn't have to get in the way
of doing what I want.
I am the one in charge of my fence.
I built it, and I am response-able
for updating it and relocating it.
It's not a question now
of what I can and I can't do.
It is a question of what I DO AND I DON'T DO.

3

**Using my results to see
I am in charge**

me: I wonder what I have put in my program.
My results are a mirror
reflecting my program to me.

Let me
re-check
my program
to see how
I got this.

I see that at times in my life
I have worked all the time
making money,
having a career.
That looks like a program I created
for me to be *like Dad*.

But then I would see that there are other
major parts of me
that I was ignoring.

Then I would feel that program wasn't right.

I should* be home taking care of my children.
I should find a husband to take care of me.
I switch over to a program I created
for me to be *like Mom*.

I spent years switching back and forth
between
conflicting partial programs,
never combining them into *one*,
revising, adding to, and deleting parts
to create
one whole program
that really works
for
all of

WHO I AM

* *Interesting word* should, *a good signal that I am trying to make* now *fit into an old program.*

I used different programs for being with
different ones of you.

I was like _____
_____
_____
with _____
I wasn't like _____
_____
_____

I was different depending on which
one of *you* I was with.

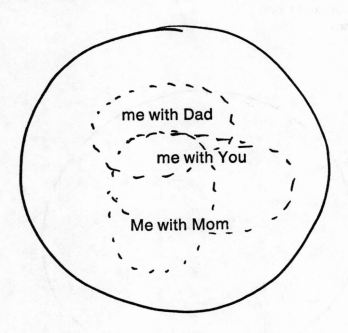

me with Dad

me with You

Me with Mom

I never really knew WHO I WAS
without *you*.

None of my partial* programs
worked for me.

* *Interesting word,* part ial.

But they were the only ones I knew,
so I used them anyway.

These partial programs were in conflict,
created by looking first from over there,
then from over there,
then over the other way;
based on how you see things, how you think,
how you feel, how you do things.

But not looking from over *here*
now,
and expanding my program for me
more and more,
into
all of

WHO I AM

What would a computer programmer do
in this situation?

Have there been signals that there were errors
in my program?
Signals in my life?

Yes. Pain, upset,
        effort, struggle,
        exhaustion
are my error messages,
my signals when there is an error in my program.

But they, *they* said, *they* taught me.
I believed that pain, upset,
effort, struggle, exhaustion
were bad, wrong,
not *signals* but *experiences to avoid*
                        to not notice
                        to overlook
                        to overcome
                        to ignore.*

They were in MY DANGER ZONE.

I have *not known* my signals,
not noticed them,
overlooked them,
overcome them,
ig-nored them,
preferring instead to continue in
what seemed to be
safe, familiar, comfortable ways,
ways I agreed with others
I *should* be.

I have operated my life
using inaccurate data,
        conflicting instructions,
        outmoded methods.

* *Interesting word,* ig-nore, *to* not know.

I have been programming my life
since the very beginning
not knowing and continuing to accumulate
more and more errors,
more and more conflicts,
like a closet full of old clothes
that no longer fit,
that I don't even like—or want—
needing to be cleaned out,
updated.

My accumulated, outmoded partial programs
don't work for me now.
The ways I was *then* don't work for me *now*.
WHO I AM is not limited, outmoded, in conflict.
But I am operating my life, me, with
limiting, outmoded, conflicting programs.

That is how I have gotten here.
That is how I have produced
the results I have.

I wonder what I could create if I used
my machine, my data, my program
free from errors
and oppositions;

if I used my signals as they were designed?

Reflecting on the computer programmer,
I see clearly that
the programmer is not his data, his information;
the programmer is not his methods, his program;
the programmer is not his computer, his machine,
or the results it produces.

The programmer is the *creator* of all that.

So too for me, the programmer of my life,
I am not what I know, my data and information;

I am not my methods, my program;
I am not my body, my machine,
or the results it produces.

I am the creator of all that.
I am all of that, **+** and **−**.

It was very confusing growing up,
hard for me to know
what I was and what I wasn't.

You said I was sick,
      I was bad or good,
         I was scared or excited,
or that's how it sounded to me.

It was not pointed out to me,
nor did I see,
that I was not sick,
but that my body was functioning in that way
to correct an *imbalance*.

Looking at it that way,
being sick is valuable feedback for me
as the programmer in charge of my body.

No one explained that
I was not good or bad,
but that my actions did not conform to the standard being
    applied.

I was not scared or excited
but *I* had learned to label
the sensations I was having in *my* body
the same way *you* labeled
the sensations you had in *your* body,
or at least you thought
they were the same.

So, based on how I've seen life so far,
I was my images,
my sound tracks, feelings, and actions.
How devastating it was for me to be wrong, bad,
for things not to turn out the way I thought;
to feel left out, or not cared about,
to have others laugh
at what I said or did.

It certainly did feel like I was my body
or maybe just my tonsils or adenoids,
looking back on how frightened I was when
they were going to be taken out.

And I felt like I was the things
I really cared about:
my brand new car dented,
my favorite dish broken,
the birthday cake I made
eaten by the dog.

And I felt like I was other people
I really care about:

my daughter hurt.
I felt like it was *me*.

And I felt like I was the things I did,
losing my first real job,
divorce ending my marriage.

I seemed no longer to exist,
my identity destroyed.

I have not understood that my machinery,
my mind and body,
my computer,
does exactly what it is told to do.
even if it is told to do two opposing things,
it will use my energy to do them both,

and that *conflict*
creates
the signals to update.

I can use my energy
to hold me back or pull me ahead,
like a mountain climber.

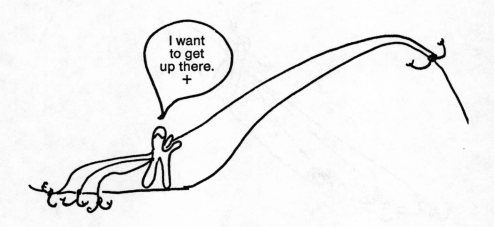

As I begin the climb, pulling up to my new anchor,
dug in where I want to go,

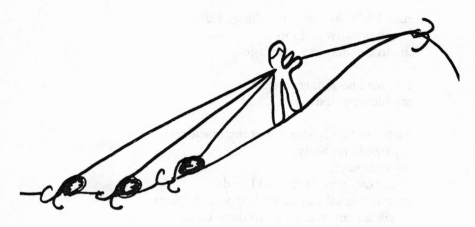

my old anchors from places I also told myself
I wanted to go
are still dug in, and they hold.
I can't make any headway.

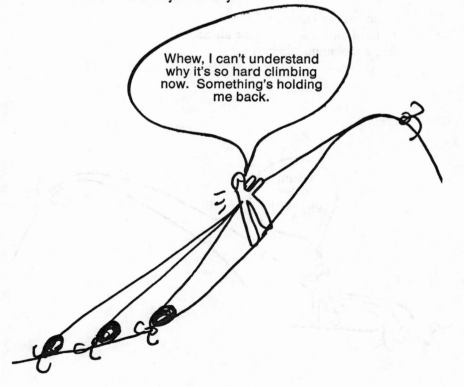

Yes, something is holding me back:
my old anchors,
my old attachments,
the ways it's comfortable, familiar, safe,
my old program statements still operating.

Interesting what I say to myself.
I took the new job but I didn't know
I'd have to work overtime,
my spouse would get so mad,
I'd have to quit bowling,
I couldn't go on the trip.
I finally had a child, but I didn't know
I wouldn't get any sleep,
it would be so hard to get out,
my life would be so different.

Pain, upset, effort, struggle, exhaustion—

my error messages
signaling me that it is time
to *update*,
to correct my conflicting instructions
so my energy is used to
produce the results
I want *now*.

I am *response-able* for *updating* my program,
adding new statements,
revising old ones,
deleting limiting, outmoded ones.

Just like updating my closet
from time to time:
looking at what I have, trying it on.
Does it fit me now?
If not, can it be altered to fit?
Have I worn this? Is it still useful to me?
Would I wear it even if I alter it?

Or is it something no longer useful,
something to delete,

making room for something new
in my life?

I am in charge of adding new goal lines,
of adjusting or cutting the old ones
I anchored in before,
still holding till I release them.

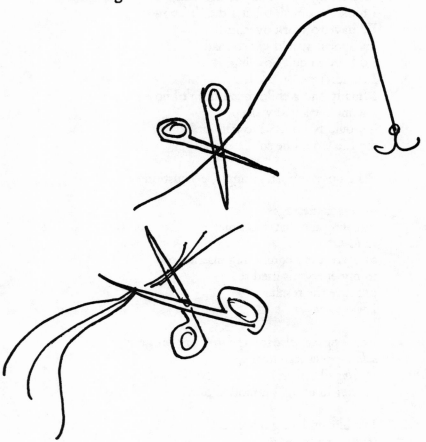

When I go *both* ways at once,
I create the signals to update,
pain, upset,
effort, struggle,
exhaustion.
I have not been response-able
till now.

I have abandoned goals when
I couldn't get them.

I have given up in anger and frustration.
I have blamed others for
my failure
to get what I wanted.

I have not seen that *I* was in charge.

4

But how did I separate *me*
from *not me*?

me: It was easy, well, no, it was very painful
to separate *me* and *you*.
How had I ever managed
to separate *me* and *not me*?
How had I separated WHO I AM

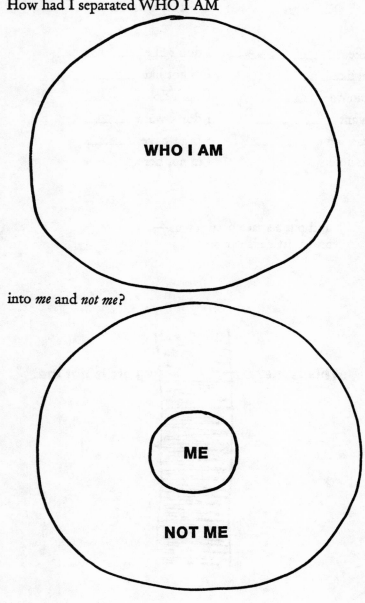

into *me* and *not me*?

I made decisions.

I created my system for keeping
me away from *not me*.

I divided everything up:

This is me   *This is not me*

I like _____   I don't like _____
I'm like _____   I'm not like _____
I can do _____   I can't do _____
I want _____   I don't want _____
I can have _____   I can't have _____
I'm here.   I'm not here.

and put a space between us—
and a little insulation.

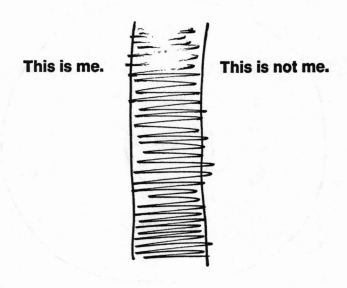

This is me.   **This is not me.**

Then I charged it.

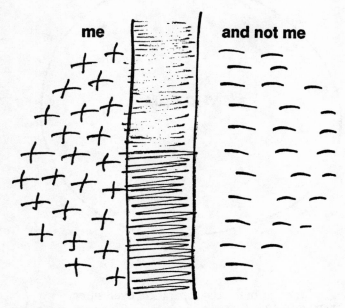

This was the fence, electrified to make it painful to get through.

WHO I AM

And then to make the separation even surer,
WHO I AM changed *not me*'s name to *you*.

Then *me* could never know *you*.
That was the only way WHO I AM could keep *me*
from finding *not me*.

Then *me* began to search for *not me*,
but the fence was in the way.
Me couldn't see *not me* except with mirrors,
and of course then everything was reversed.
That made *not me* hard for *me* to recognize.

And if *me* was attracted over to *not me*,
me couldn't recognize *not me*
because *not me*'s name had been changed to *you*,
and they hadn't seen each other since birth.

So then *me* could find *you*
but not *not me*.

And that's how WHO I AM accomplished
the separation of WHO I AM.

Now that *me* knows how WHO I AM was separated,
how can *me* put WHO I AM back together again?

It may sound easy, but it's been very painful so far.

Me is connected to a body that grows
and is constantly changing.
As soon as *me* figures out something
about *me*, me's system,
it changes,
making it hard for *me* even to figure out *me*,
much less *not me*.

And *not me*, now called *you*, is divided up
into four billion pieces.
The charge helps.
If *me* knows it's missing something,
then *me*'s automatically attracted
to part of *not me*.

But *me* keeps thinking that what's missing
is one piece,
me's other half.
Looking one piece at a time,
it could take forever for *me*
to find out WHO I AM.

And *me*'s system was made up very early in life
before *me* had much chance to find many pieces.
The more pieces *me* finds,
the easier it is for *me* to begin to figure out
how WHO I AM all fits together.
All of *you* fit together in *not me*,
$$\frac{\text{and all those} \quad (4 \text{ billion} - \text{one) pieces} \quad + \text{me}}{\text{is}}$$

WHO I AM

All of *you* fit together in *not me*. And all those
4 billions minus one pieces, plus *me*, is equal to
WHO I AM.

And all the divorces between *me* and *you*
are just feedback
that adding

$$\frac{\text{1 of you} + \text{1 of me}}{}$$
does not equal

WHO I AM

Me can only truly marry *not me*.
Then I am *me* and I am *not me*.
I am all there is,
everything.
And I can love *you*
and be with any part of
WHO I AM.

Now at last, *me* sees
me has misunderstood about feelings,
about the ZAP.
The ZAP is WHO I AM signaling me
to be alert, to wake up!
This is part of WHO I AM,
a part *me* has not recognized,
me has not found.

PAY ATTENTION, ME.

Me is on the brink of discovery.
Me is about to discover another piece of
WHO I AM.

MY DANGER ZONE really is dangerous,
dangerous for me to avoid,
for without discovering *me* in there,
I cannot be all of WHO I AM.

So now that we know the game
and how it is,
let's write out the instructions,
the manual for being human.

5

A word from your maker

me: But somewhere inside I knew,
I knew I knew.

Somehow I knew I had always been seated
at the controls of my own ship
steering and guiding my life.
I had known I was the one who had to discover
how to use all the lights and buzzers
on my control panel,
that I was the one in charge of
setting my course,
of communicating to others about my ship,
my location, my needs,
what I saw from my position in space.

But I had been overwhelmed from the start.
It was too much.

I had begun my career as an apprentice pilot
with a mother ship beside me,
with another pilot over there
talking me through my early flights,
assisting me in steering and monitoring,
telling me how he flew his ship,
what he knew about how his ship operated.

In the beginning I had known that
his ship was a different model.
His ship operated in many of the same ways,
but it was not the same.

He would be there for a while
till I figured out how to fly my ship,
and then he'd leave.

He had been a little unsure when we set out
because he said he wasn't entirely familiar
with my model,
but he thought it operated pretty much like his.

And I remember noticing
that sometimes he would call over to my ship
that a certain light should be
on my control panel on my right,
but it was on my left.
I noticed that.

Sometimes he would describe what he saw
out of his window.
It was not the same
as what I saw out of mine.
I noticed that.

But it had been safe listening to him.
I had been steering along OK.
And I had begun to listen more and more
to him,
and I paid less and less attention
to my own lights and buzzers.
They only seemed to confuse me.

I was never sure I understood my ship.
Lights and buzzers would come on from time to time
that weren't on his panel
or were in a different position.
I would be confused by them,
and he would tell me what to do.

It was frustrating trying to do things
his way
and at the same time
trying to figure out how all that
related to my system.

I began to disregard my lights and buzzers,
and to listen more and more
to what he told me.

Occasionally my lights and buzzers
would really annoy me.

I would start to doubt what he was saying.
I would get confused and upset.
One time I had a crash when I was distracted
by all that.
After that I was afraid.

I decided that the best thing for my safety
was to cover my lights
and disconnect my buzzers,
and listen only to what others told me to do.

At last it was calm and quiet;
however, there always remained a feeling down deep
that I had done the wrong thing,
that there was something missing,
some reason for those lights and buzzers.

It was much simpler now,
but what if he ever left me?
What if I ever had to fly entirely on my own?

I wish I had a manual for operating me.
I wish I had talked to my maker
about how I worked,
what everything meant,
how to use all of the signals I have built into my ship,

It had been easy following along,
but I must learn about me on my own.
I am going to uncover my control panel,
my lights and buzzers.
I am going to explore their use
and write for me a manual
for how to operate me.

I can ask others.
I can see the similarities and differences,
but I know that
I am the only one in charge,
the only one who knows about me.

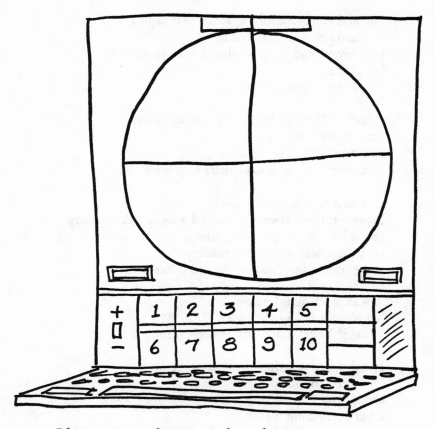

I have uncovered my control panel.
What does all this mean?

This is scary, uncomfortable, and
so was the other way.
I am going to figure it out this time.

There's a light blinking on my control console.

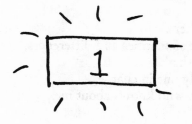

I'll push it and see what happens. A voice.

Voice: WHAT DO YOU WANT?

me: What did you say?

Voice: WHAT DO YOU WANT?

me: Well, I guess that *is* number 1.
What do I want?
I'm in charge now, so I'd better figure
out where I'm going.
First things first:
What do I see is ahead for me?

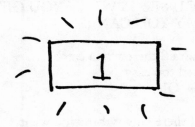

There's the voice again.

Voice: CREATE A CLEAR AND COMPLETE PICTURE
OF WHAT YOU WANT, USING ALL YOU KNOW.

me: OK, I got it, using all I know. I see.
Yeah, that's it. I need *to see* what I want.
I want to _____
I can see me doing it now.
Wow, this is exciting. I'm in charge.

Voice: Remember, WHAT YOU SEE IS WHAT YOU GET.

me: What I see is what I get. OK.
I'm clear now on WHAT I WANT.
I can see it clearly. I've even
imagined little details about how
this is for me. I can see *me* doing it now.

Voice: Good. You have finished Phase 1 of creating.
Push sequence light 2.

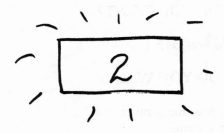

WHAT YOU SEE IS WHAT YOU GET, IF YOU SAY YOU CAN.

me: Oh, I was afraid there was a catch.
It just seemed too easy.
If I say I can. OK.

Voice: See yourself there now, where you want
to be, and tell yourself you'll get there
from here. Get back to me when you have your plan.

me: Yes, I am in charge. I do have to talk over
my method, the route I'll take
from here to there.
I'll have to _____
I'll need to _____
I think I'll want to _____
I'd better find out _____

It sounds like I can do it.
OK, I have my plan.

Voice: Good
WHAT YOU SEE IS WHAT YOU GET,
AND NOW YOU SAY YOU CAN.

me: Yes, I say I can. I'm so glad you're here.
Everything's going so smoothly.
I'm beginning to think about things more clearly.
What's next?

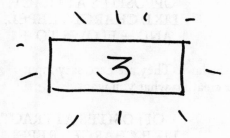

Voice: Good.
WHAT YOU SEE IS WHAT YOU GET.
WHEN YOU SAY YOU CAN,
THEN YOU'LL FEEL YOU CAN.

me: Oh yes, feelings, I was sure that would
come up. I've got a charge about feelings.

Voice: Yes, feelings really are just
the charge you place on things.
YOU ARE IN CHARGE OF YOUR FEELINGS.
YOU ARE IN CHARGE OF THE CHARGE,
whether you see and say things are + or − ,
whether you see and say you are + or − ,
whether you see and say others are + or − .
+ or − . Neither one is better than the other.
Both are necessary.

me: Well, I see what you're saying, if I'm looking
at a battery. There it's obvious. There is
no flow without + and − connected up. I guess
I've always felt − was bad, not just − .

Voice: Yes, that's so. But now you know.
YOU ARE IN CHARGE OF YOUR CHARGE.

me: But what does that have to do with getting
what I want?

Voice: Good question. That's where the laws of the
physical universe come in. They apply to you
too you know.

OPPOSITES ATTRACT,
LIKE CHARGES REPEL,
AND − FLOWS TO + .

Repeat the laws. They are necessary input
for your creating what you want.

me:

OPPOSITES ATTRACT,
LIKE CHARGES REPEL,
AND − FLOWS TO + .

Yes, I learned that in school, but it was
never very useful to me.

Voice: TILL NOW. In your life you have done a lot with + and − ,
though you didn't observe your doing that. You
have divided you into two parts: + and − .

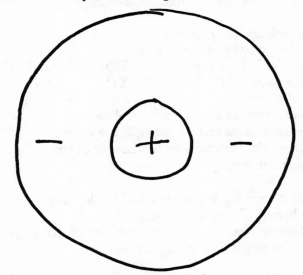

And you have learned to switch charges
back and forth.
Do you see the switch on your left?

me: Yes.

Voice: That's your manual polarity control,
if you ever need it.
Did you get that? Repeat.

me: Yes, that's my manual polarity control—for what?

Voice: For switching from − to + , or + to − .
Look at your viewer now.

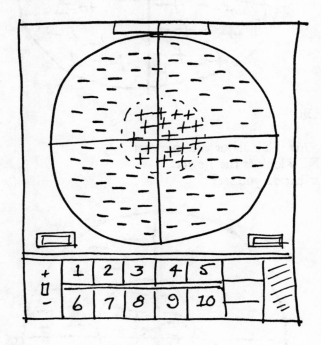

Do you see that small area in the center?
That's where you have set your limits.
You have said you must stay in there.
That's where it's safe, familiar,
where you know you can.

That's what you call *me*.

Now let go of your point of view for
a minute, and the viewer will show you
the way it is with no point of view.

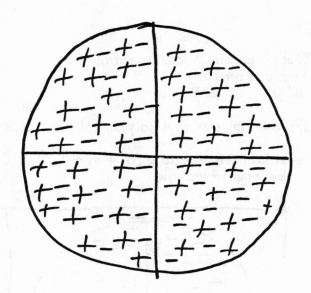

me: Oh.

Voice: Now think about your part-ner.
Now look at the viewer.
What do you see?

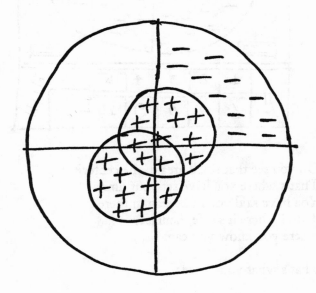

me: Me. No, *him*, his me, the way he limits
his territory.

Voice: Now think of you. *Your me* will appear on the viewer. OK. Now see how the two *me*'s fit together.

me: Yes, I see. We each have been in charge of our charges, where *me* is, whether it seemed more like *me*

to see it as **+** or **−** ,
to say it is **+** or **−** ,
to feel it is **+** or **−** ,
to do **+** or **−** .
So out of all of it, everything,

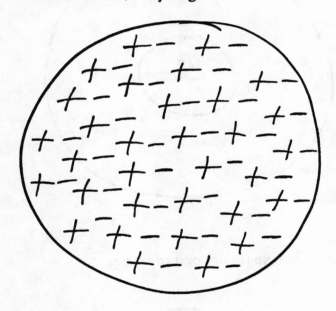

each of us *de cided* where is *me*,
where is *not me*,
where are *you*.
And then attracted the **+** charges to *me*
and repelled the **−** charges from *me*.

Voice: Yes. And you have learned to switch that *me* area from **+** to **−** .

me: I have? When do I do that?

Voice: Sometimes you say:

"I see what I want,
I tell myself I'll get it,
I feel I'll get it,
I do what it takes.
And I get it. +"

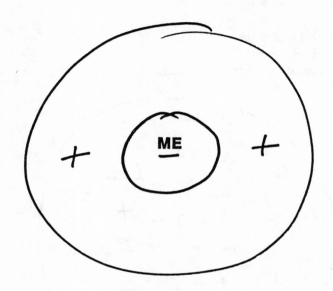

Other times you switch over to saying:

"I see what I don't want,
I tell myself I'll get what I don't want,
I feel I'll get what I don't want,
I do things not to get it.
And I get it. — "

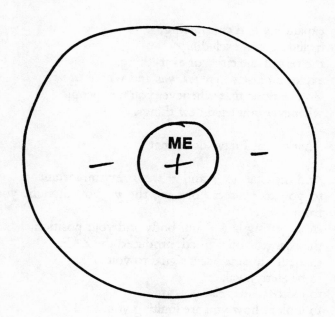

me: Oh yes, I know both of those
situations well.
I see what you mean now.

Voice: All of your life you have experimented with

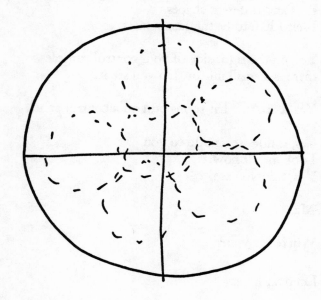

expanding and contracting,
including and excluding
the rest of the circle of everything,
exploring just where *me* was and where *me* wasn't.
You've done that whenever you met people,
whenever you tried new things.

me: That's true. I have done that.

Voice: And the charges + and − were very important
to you to protect your *me*, the *me* you thought you were,
from danger,
from getting hurt. Your body and your position,
the charges you created, produced the ZAP,
that current acted as a signal to you
to be alert, awake,
to look at what else you are,
to look at how you are limiting you.
But you were afraid, and you didn't see it that way.
You saw it as a fence,
a boundary around that *me* part of WHO YOU ARE,
as a signal to stay *inside* where it was safe, familiar.

me: Yes, I did, and it sure made it difficult to
explore changing *me* around, making *me* different
sizes and different shapes.
I felt I had to be the same.

Voice: Yes, on the right side of your control console
there is a small mirror. Do you see it?

me: Yes, I see it. That seems odd on a control panel.

Voice: Yes, it does seem odd to you.
Look into it now.
What do you see?

me: Me.

Voice: Where are you?

me: I'm over here.

Voice: Look again in the mirror. Where are you?

me: Oh, I'm over *there*.

Voice: Good. You're beginning to really find out where you are.
Whenever you get upset with your ship
or with others you communicate with,
that come near you,
LOOK IN THE MIRROR to remind yourself that
you are over there,
that you see yourself over *there*,
that you are seeing in a mirror all the time.
It is valuable feedback,
feedback you'll need in order to
UPDATE your position,
the size and shape of your *me*,
to UPDATE your limits.
YOU LIMIT YOURSELF. YOU ALWAYS HAVE.

me: I limit myself. I always have.
Yeah, I've noticed that from time to time,
like when I said,
"I can't imagine that, I can't say that,
feel that, do that, have that."
I have always limited *me*,
but it looked like *you* limited me,
like the *world* limited me.

Voice: Yes. Remember the mirror. Where are you?

me: Yes, I have always limited *me*.

Voice: Now that you know that,
you can begin to use
the Laws of the Universe
to your *ad-vantage*.*

me: How can I do that?

Voice: Repeat the Laws.

* *Interesting*, ad-vantage, *to add to the opportunity*.

me: OPPOSITES ATTRACT
LIKE CHARGES REPEL.
AND + FLOWS TO − .

Voice: Good. Now you can begin. Have you noticed that whenever you

said you felt you lacked something, or you *wanted* something, that you *got* something?

me: Yes, I've noticed that.
Like when I was searching for my other half
and I found my part-ner.
We were very attracted.

Voice: Ah, you noticed that too.
Now do you see how the law applies?
You said you were missing something.

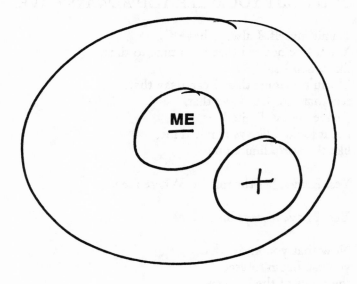

You put a *negative* charge on your *me*,
and so you automatically attracted
a *positive* part to you.

me: But how did I know that it was a positive part?

Voice: You didn't really know. But you saw
he knows what I don't,
he does what I can't,
he has what I don't.
You saw him as positive, and then
the laws just naturally took over
and — was attracted to + .
Do you remember that now?

me: Oh yes, I see. I never looked at it that way.
I AM IN CHARGE OF MY CHARGE, MY FEELINGS,
OF WHAT I ATTRACT AND WHAT I REPEL.
If I want, I need, I see me as — .
If I can do, I have, I see me as + .
If you want, you need, I see you as — .
If you can do, you have, I see you as + .
I have really been the one in charge of
what I got, who I got,
of what happened to me all along.

Voice: When you become a little more *neutral*,
you will not be so at the mercy of the
physical laws,
so suddenly attracted and suddenly repelled.

me: Yes, that would be nice.

Voice: Are you clear that
WHAT YOU SEE IS WHAT YOU GET?
WHEN YOU SAY YOU CAN,
THEN YOU'LL FEEL YOU CAN?

me: Yes.

Voice: And that YOU ARE IN CHARGE OF YOUR CHARGE,
of your feelings,
WHAT IS ATTRACTED TO YOU AND REPELLED
FROM YOU?

me: Yes, I see that clearly.
Tell me more about creating.

Voice: OK. If you see yourself there,
and there is **+** , what you want,
then that part of you that is *here*
will naturally be attracted
to *there*.

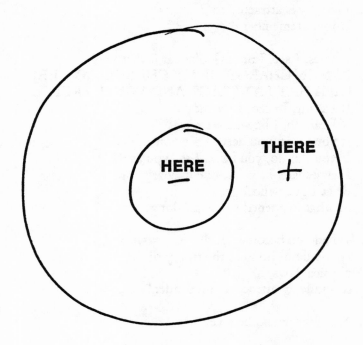

You see your creative energy flows along
a circuit.
Repeat the laws now.

me: OPPOSITES ATTRACT.
LIKE CHARGES REPEL.
AND − FLOWS TO **+** .

Voice: OK.
Look at your viewer
at the top, **+/−** .
Which way will the energy flow?

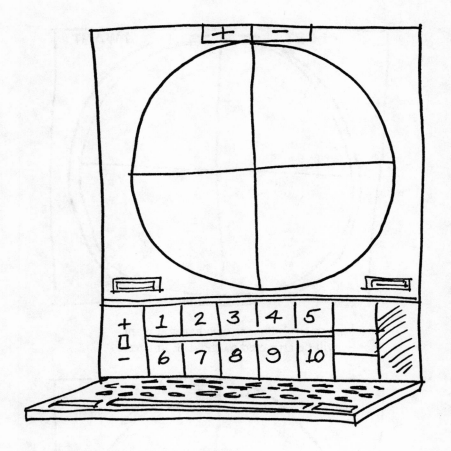

me: The law says − flows to + .

Voice: Good, that is how it is.
So your negative energy, your wanting energy,
will just naturally be attracted to I GET,
and will flow around to + .
Do you see that on your control panel?

me: Yes.

Voice: Let's look at that flow so far.

WHAT YOU SEE IS WHAT YOU GET.
WHEN YOU SAY YOU CAN,
THEN YOU'LL FEEL YOU CAN.

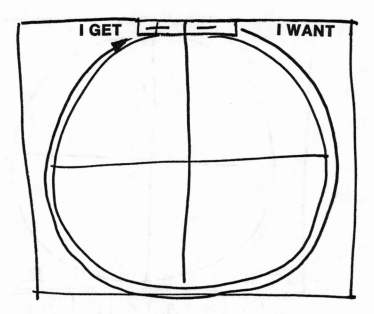

So when you see **+** images of what you want,
that **−** will be attracted to those **+** images.

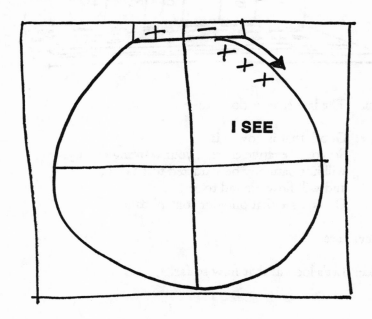

As long as the images are **+**, the energy will just naturally flow
along the I SEE phase, and on to what I SAY.

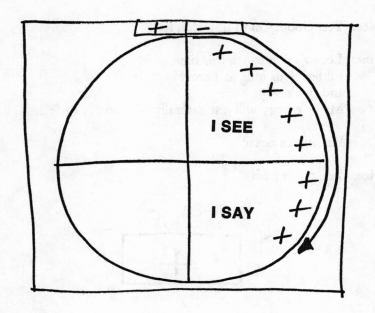

As long as you think +ly about that + image, the energy will just naturally be attracted to your + thinking all the way along the thinking phase as you flow on to

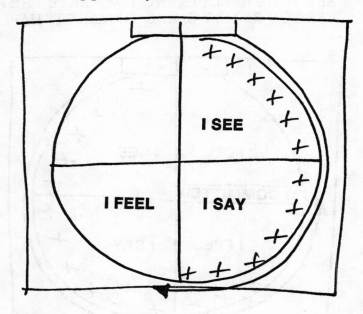

me: That part's how I feel about what I want.

Voice: Yes. Good. On to how you feel.

me: Let *me* tell it to *you* this time.
I'll feel + as long as I see +ly
and think +ly.
My − energy will just naturally flow to . . . to . . . .

But what's next?

Voice: Yes, on to push

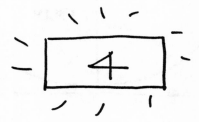

There's an important decision that has
to be made here.
ARE YOU REALLY GOING TO CREATE THIS?
ARE YOU REALLY GOING TO MAKE IT HAPPEN?

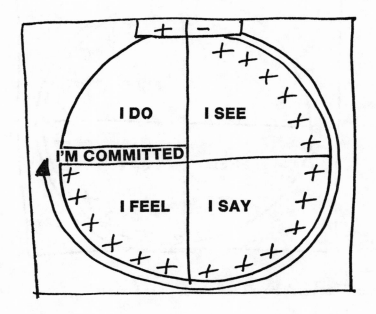

Are you ready to commit to doing this?
WHAT YOU SEE IS WHAT YOU GET.
WHEN YOU SAY YOU CAN,
THEN YOU'LL FEEL YOU CAN,
AND YOU'LL DO WHATEVER IT TAKES TO GET
    IT.

Are you really going to use this program you have been
    developing?
Is it GO or NO GO?
Time for ignition, for blasting off
to that imagined destination.
Once the program is in the mechanism, it's GO.
The energy is committed to create this,
one way or the other.
There will be many corrections, updates, along the way.
But the holding orbit is over.
Action begins, blasting you off into space.
You begin doing whatever it takes
to make this image real, to get there,
not just see there.

me: WAIT. I have a few doubts, a few thoughts
    that maybe I can't, a feeling that maybe
    it won't work out OK.

Voice: Good, you noticed them. You are doing very well.
    Push the next phase.

Have any negatives crept in
along the circuit so far,
slowing down the flow,
the energy to go ahead?

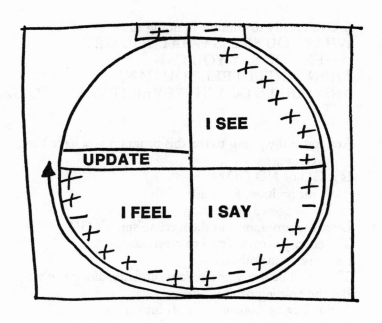

Voice: You have made up a program for creating
your image, for creating what you want.
Now you must de-bug it.
You must work out those —es.
It is time to UPDATE.

What did you see that was — ?
What did you think that was — ?
Those — feelings are signals of —es in your circuit.
What does — mean?

me: I used to think it meant bad, wrong,
not for *me*.

Voice: Does it mean that still?
Even though you can't see you succeeding at something,
can you see others succeeding at it?

me: Yes, they're different.
They have different systems.

Voice: Exactly. Their *me* is in a different position
amongst everything, or their *me* is more movable,
able to expand and shift according to what they want.

To create what you want, you'll have to be able
to expand your *me* to include
whatever it takes to create what you want.

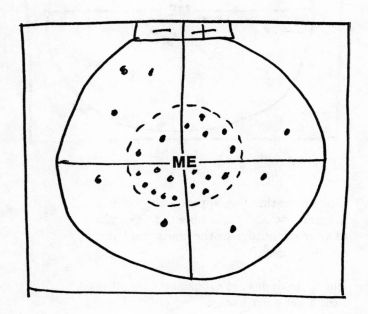

You'll have to expand your images of *me*.
You'll have to expand *me*'s thinking
You'll have to allow *me* to have new feelings.
You'll have to do new things, things your *me* hasn't included.
You'll have to expand your *me* to include
whatever it takes to create what you want.

So what does — mean now?

me: Negative for me is anything *I can't*,
anything I say is *not me*, is outside of *me*.

Voice: Look at your viewer now.

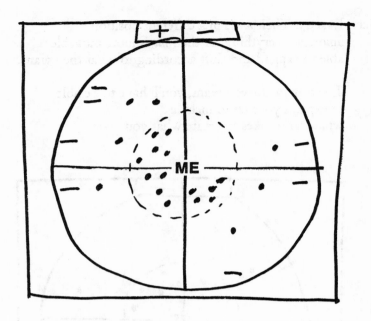

Do you see that −es appear wherever your
program includes something that is outside
of your *me*, outside of the limits you have
set for yourself?

   me: But those things are *not* like *me*.
          I can't get what I want
          if I have to. . . .

Voice: Who says you can't?

   me: Who? Well, I . . . I do. I guess that's really how
          it is, isn't it?

Voice: Yes, that's how it is.

   me: Oh, that's what you said. I limit myself.
          I always have.

Voice: Can you now expand into any direction to get what you want?
          It all depends on how you see it, how dangerous it is, or how
          much you want it.

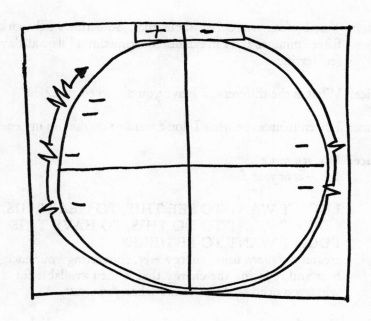

Is it safe now to only be the way you have always been, allowing only others to imagine what it takes, to think what it takes, to feel what it takes, to do everything it takes to get what *you* want?

me: NO. It's not. I want to get what I want.
I am willing to expand *me*, to allow *me* to be more flexible.

Voice: That's what it will take.

me: But I don't always know when I have —es in my circuit.

Voice: Yes you do.
Negatives in your circuit create *resistance, heat.*
Have you noticed that?

me: Heat. You mean I get hot?

Voice: Yes, hot and bothered, hot under the collar, hotheaded, in a sweat.
Resistance is very useful for heating a cockpit when it's cold, but resistance *reduces the energy* that can flow onto what you want.

me: Yes, I often wondered about that. Sometimes I'll work for fifteen minutes and I'm exhausted. Sometimes I'll go all day and feel terrific.

Voice: What is the difference? Have you observed that?

me: Fifteen minutes of what I don't want to do uses up my energy.

Voice: Yes, *resistance*
puts —es in your flow.

I DON'T WANT TO SEE THIS, TO HEAR THIS.
I DON'T WANT TO DO THIS, TO HAVE THIS.
I DON'T WANT TO BE HERE,
creates *resistance*, using energy —ly, converting your energy to heat and reducing the energy that is then available for doing what you need to do to create what you want.

me: Does that have anything to do with losing speed? Losing momentum?

Voice: Yes. As you slow down your energy you lose momentum. That produces heat, resistance, sort of like re-entry.

me: So if I'm slowing *me* down, then I'll feel that heat, the heat of my resistance.

Voice: Yes, good. *Heat is a signal of resistance.* And if you're really *hot* with somebody else, don't forget the mirror.

me: Oh. I see what you mean.

Voice: Now notice the three indicators on your right.

HEAT
ENERGY
SPEED

You'll be using more energy to produce the same results if you don't update the —es, if you leave them in your creative circuit. You're liable to run out of energy before you get there, lost in space.

That's just how it is.

When you see the *low energy* light on, check also on your temperature. Are you overheating, using energy for resistance? Your update light will come on then.

HEAT and LOW ENERGY are signals to UPDATE *immediately*.

If you use up your energy in resistance, you run the risk of running out of energy, losing power, of your engines shutting down,

losing momentum,
being overcome by inertia,
negativity,
confusion,
coldness/numbness,
unconsciousness.

me: I think I've got it now.
  WHAT I SEE IS WHAT I GET WHEN

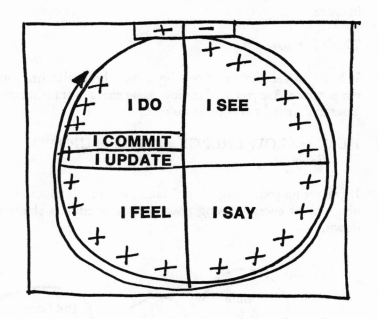

But wait. I don't know whether I'll know
what to do. Maybe I won't be able to do it.

Voice: The word *but* is a signal that there are −es
in your circuit. Remember, WHAT YOU SEE ...

me: Yes, WHAT I SEE IS WHAT I GET.
  Oops! I'm in trouble.
  No, I'm in need of an UPDATE
  to clear those −es
  that are coming up now.
  But I don't know how to do everything yet.
  I don't know how to steer.
  Where's my steering wheel?

Voice: Oh, yes, I guess that's how you're used to steering.
  No, there's a different system used on this ship.
  That's where the polarity switch comes in.

It's really an electrical system,
a system of approach,
avoidance through attraction and repulsion.
IF YOU SEE YOU WANT TO APPROACH IT, it is **+**
   for now.
YOU WILL JUST NATURALLY APPROACH IT.
IF YOU SEE YOU WANT TO AVOID IT, it is **−**
   for now.
YOU WILL JUST NATURALLY BE REPELLED BY IT.
That's how you have always steered through life.

me: It really is, but I didn't look at it that way. I thought I had to
always go in a straight line. I had to be careful to do this first,
then that, then this, then that.

Voice: Did that ever work?

me: No, no it didn't. I just felt like a failure most of the time.
I would start off straight for it,
1 2 3 4 5 6 7 8 9 10
then when I couldn't *do* 5 I would get really upset.
I couldn't do it.
I couldn't get there.
I failed.
I would see me failing, feeling miserable, not getting what
I wanted.

Voice: Yes, it started out fine.
You saw what you wanted.
You thought how you would get it.
You felt you could.
You committed to getting it.
You started doing.

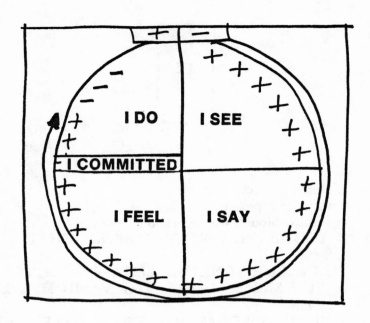

But then it got hard,
not the way you pictured it.
The old ways started looking better and better—

"I'm better off where I was before."

So instead of *updating* and *expanding* or *adjusting,*
you *switched polarity.*
And then your − energy just naturally flowed toward **+** ,
and you headed back to where you were—

"I couldn't *do* it.
It never *felt* right, anyway.
I *told myself* I would have problems.
I *see* it wasn't really so good, after all—"

justifying the retreat as you go back
to where you started.

Can you remember using that switch before?

me: Oh yes, *many* times, many many times,
but I never knew how that all worked.
I just found myself back there where
it was safe, familiar.

Voice: Yes, the physical laws always apply,
inexorably.

me: Yes, but sometimes the very things I most
feared would happen did happen.
I would see how horrible it would be if that ever
happened.
I just couldn't get it *out of my mind.*

Voice: *Out of your creative cycle* you mean.
You create in your mind
and then do it with your body.
The body gets all those images and thoughts
you put into it,
and then your body starts to get ready
for what you have told it is ahead.
IF YOU SHOW YOUR BODY +ES, IT WILL
   RESPOND +LY,

eagerly,
enthusiastically,
flowing easily, building up speed, momentum
for what's ahead.

IF YOU SHOW YOUR BODY —ES, IT WILL
   RESPOND —LY,
getting ready for the —es you see,
the —es you say
are ahead.

If you show your body both +es *and* −es,
it will, like the computer, respond to
both inputs, creating resistance,
opposing energy flows.

Your body will signal you, the programmer,
through its ALERT messages:

PAIN, UPSET,
EFFORT, STRUGGLE,
EXHAUSTION.

Don't forget **5** to UPDATE

WHAT YOU SEE IS WHAT YOU GET.
WHEN YOU SAY YOU CAN,
THEN YOU'LL FEEL YOU CAN.

That applies whether you see and think
+ or − .
SO IT PAYS
TO SEE AND SAY WHAT YOU WANT.
THEN YOU'LL FEEL YOU CAN,
AND YOU'LL DO WHATEVER IT TAKES.

me: Whatever it takes?

Voice: Yes, whatever it takes.
What else has been more important to you than what you
wanted?

me: Well, being comfortable,
safe, liked.

Voice: Ah, you noticed. Very good.

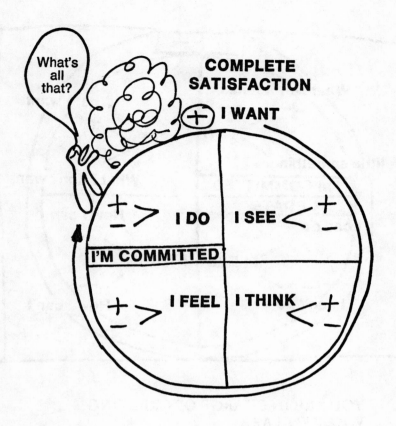

If you only do a little
but not whatever it takes
to get what you want,
you have added another incompletion
to the already accumulated
pile of INCOMPLETIONS

between you and WHAT YOU WANT,

between you and COMPLETION,

between you and SATISFACTION.

You are the one who chooses.

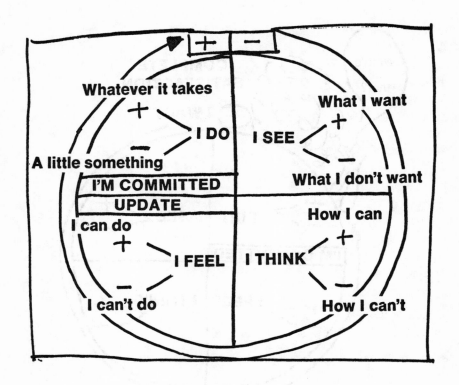

YOU ARE IN CHARGE OF CREATING
WHAT YOU ARE.

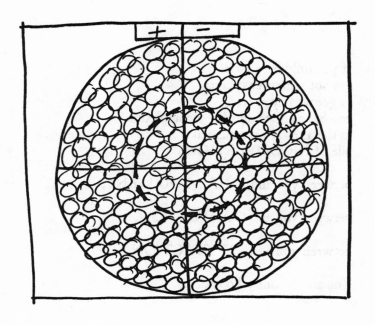

This is how all your energy is invested:
everything you see you are doing
and you are not doing,

everything you think about,
everything you don't think about,

everything you feel
and you don't feel,

everything you are doing
and you are not doing.

When you complete a cycle,
that *energy release*
propels you ahead
to WHAT'S NEXT.

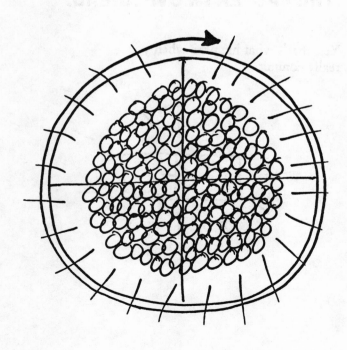

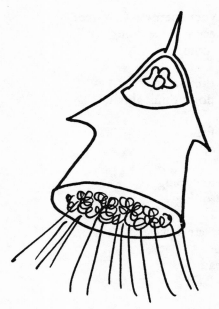

I SAID I WOULD, I DID.
I SAID I WOULD, I DID.
THE MORE MOMENTUM I CREATE,
THE FASTER I MOVE AHEAD.

Yes, that's what happens when you
really commit.

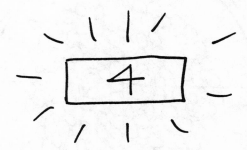

6

Going on Internal Guidance

me: WHEW!
When I got everything updated,
and I saw and told myself I could,
I felt READY TO COMMIT.
My system reallys works when
I *work it.*

I'm doing everything smoothly.
Time for an UPDATE.

Have any negatives crept into my circuit?

My ship is perfectly designed.

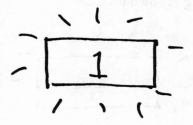

I see what I want—clearly, completely, +ly.

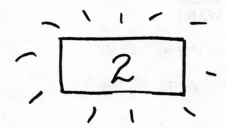

I must think what I need to do to get it.
How far have I come?
Where am I now along the way?
What corrections do I have to make
to continue heading for what I want?

OK. I've made all the corrections I can see now.
I have updated my course.

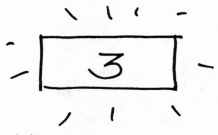

How do I feel?
I feel energetic,
enthusiastic,
ready to get WHAT I WANT.
What the Voice says works.
Interesting. *I'm hearing it in my head now.*
I know exactly how it is,
how I was designed and made.
I am creating my own manual.

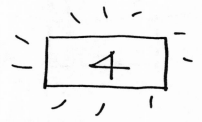

Yes, I'm committed to getting
WHAT I WANT.

Voice: You're doing very well indeed.

me: Yes, I am doing very well indeed.

The UPDATE light has stopped blinking.

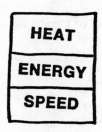

All OK.

This looks somewhat different from what I expected.

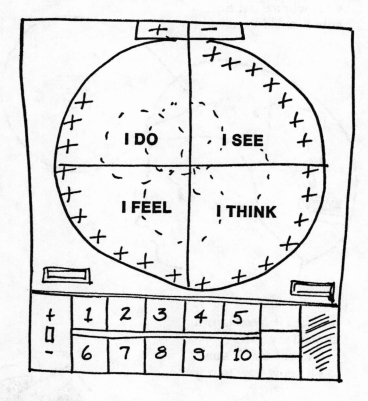

My *me* keeps moving around on my viewer.
First it expands toward seeing more.
Then it expands into
hearing when I'm hearing,
doing when I'm doing.
My *me* is not always the same;
I never had any way to see that before.

My view is not just of what's outside,
of what's ahead;
My viewer also shows what's inside,
what's before.

I see something out there,
and I *automatically* compare it
to something I see inside my head.
I try to figure out
what it's like,
how it turned out before,
what worked last time,
how I should handle it now.

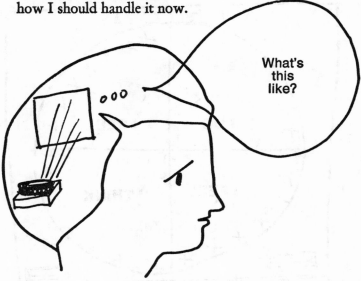

It's like I *automatically* run
through my slides
to find one that is similar
so I'll know how to respond.

I am like my computer.
That's how it works,
relying on its memory
of what to do under similar circumstances,
how to respond if . . . .

Sometimes the slide I compare it to
is a disaster;
then I say something horrible is coming up.

When I show myself that slide,
I say, yes, it's going to be like this.
I automatically tell my body
how to respond,
what to be ready for.

And it starts immediately adjusting
the speed slower, the temperature higher,
firing opposing thrusters to slow the ship down,
to avoid what's ahead.
I'm scared, nervous,
tense, warm.

But wait . . . .
It really isn't the way I used to see it.
It's not I FEEL SO I DO.
My feelings don't cause my behavior.

What I show me—the slide I show myself
of what I see ahead—
that's how I create my feelings.

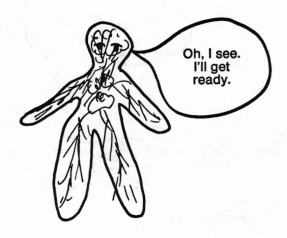

Oh, I see.
I'll get
ready.

I do have *control* over my feelings,
the electricity in my fence.
I am in *charge* of my feelings.

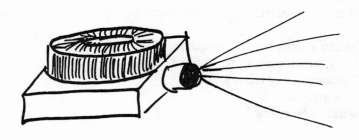

I am the *projectionist*.

I am the one who selects the view
that I will show my body
to get ready for. . . .

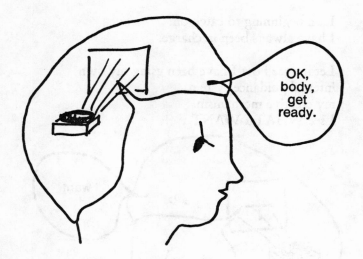

I must have a lot of disaster slides
in my collection.

I think it's time to UPDATE
my view of life.

Since what I see is what I get.

I want to see things working out for me.
I want to see me getting WHAT I WANT.

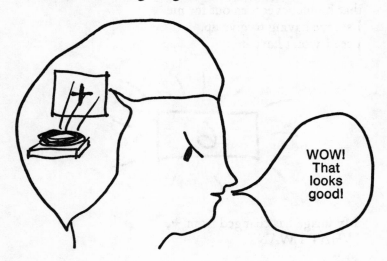

I haven't done that.

I am beginning to catch on.
I have always been in charge.

Let me see how I have been using my own
internal guidance system,
my creative mechanism.
I see WHAT I WANT.   **+**

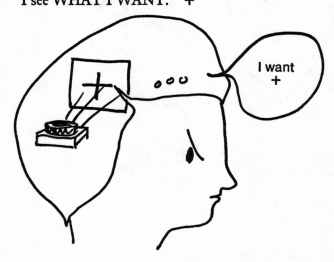

But wait. What's happening?
I've lost that image.
Now I'm seeing that I CAN'T GET IT,
that it will never turn out for me.
I see me having to give up.
I see I won't have it.

My image has changed from **+**,
WHAT I WANT,
to **−**,
WHAT I DON'T WANT.

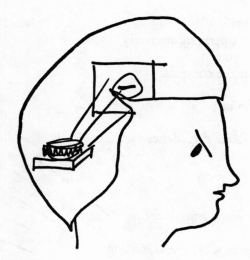

What happened? I seem to be on
automatic.

AUTOMATIC NEGATIVE.

If I keep focusing on − ,
that will be what I will get.

There must be
something wrong
with my ship.

Voice: Nothing's wrong.
Your ship is operating perfectly,
given what you
are doing at the controls.

me: I'm back on my
negative
automatic internal guidance system.

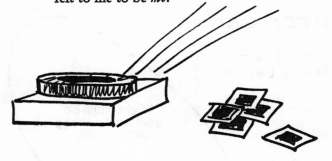

I'm seeing things negatively.

I'm looking at what else is missing,
the things I left behind, my old life,
safe, familiar ways, the way it always
felt to me to be *me*.

But WHAT I SEE IS WHAT I'LL GET.

Look out . . . .
I'm heading for all that old stuff.

I'm on AUTOMATIC, heading directly for it.

I'm in trouble!

Voice: No, not in trouble, only in need of an UPDATE.
Go back to number

See +ly what you want.
Create a clear and complete image,
using *all you know* to your ad-vantage.

You are using what you know against you,
to your dis-advantage,
comparing NOW with the past—NOT NOW.

You will attract your − wanting energy
right back to where you were.

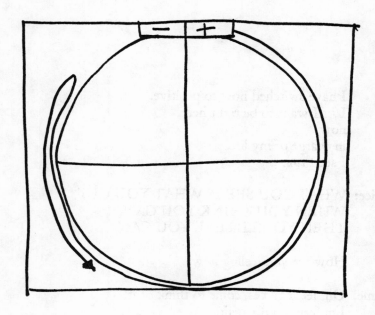

Is that what you want now?
If it is, continue.
You will then have updated
and be back on course to where you were.

me: *No, That is not what I want.*
I see now. I was back into my old ways.
I was on automatic—AUTOMATIC NEGATIVE.

I think it's time for that switch.

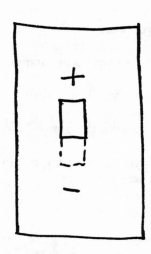

I have switched now to positive.
I *see* I want to be right here,
now,
in charge of my life.
I see I *can*.

Voice: WHAT YOU SEE IS WHAT YOU GET.
WHEN YOU THINK YOU CAN,
THEN YOU'LL FEEL YOU CAN.

How are you feeling now?

me: Oh, feeling. Yes, come to think of it,
I'm feeling GO again.
I feel committed.
I'm updated and back on course.
I feel positive now.

Voice: Yes, there's nothing wrong with your ship.

me: I know. I am the one at the controls.
I AM THE ONE IN CHARGE.

I had developed a lot of habits
that don't work.

I need to observe everything
very carefully
and be prepared to switch to manual,

when I see I'm using my internal guidance system
in the old un-workable way.
I like being in charge.
I'm getting WHAT I WANT now.

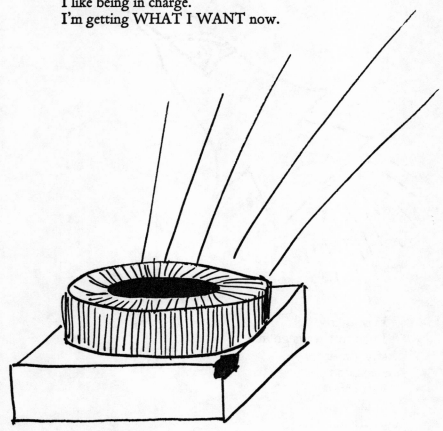

I am the PROJECTIONIST in charge of
HOW I SEE LIFE.

Things are looking good.

I used to think
I had to steer
very carefully.

I thought
I had to always go in a
straight line.
I couldn't
veer off
at all,
or else . . .

I would see me crashing and burning.

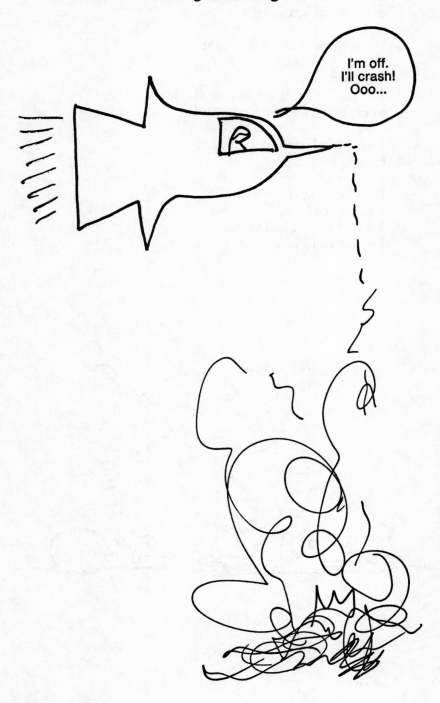

I didn't have any freedom to look around
or check out anything new.

I always had to do it just right
or
I felt bad.
I would see I was headed for disaster,
so my body would get prepared.

I would feel nervous, tight,
bracing for disaster.

If I got off at all,
I would see I had failed,
I would think I had failed,
I would feel I had failed.

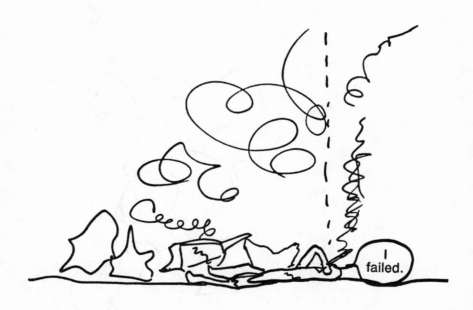

I always wanted to *be* correct,
not
to correct.

CORRECTIONAL
INSTITUTION

I thought correction
meant punishment.
I was afraid of correction.

Now I see the only way that works
is to correct, to UPDATE.

Oops!
Out a
little.

Oops!
I'm off.
I see + .

Oops!
Too much.

I don't have to steer a straight course.
In fact, that is something I rarely do.

I don't have to do it right.
There is no *right*.
I only have to keep seeing WHAT I WANT
and keep watching and correcting.

I have an audience,
in fact, two audiences—
the one *outside* of me,
what you say about me,
and the one *inside* my head,
what *I* say about me.

I'm afraid you might say the things
I think about me.

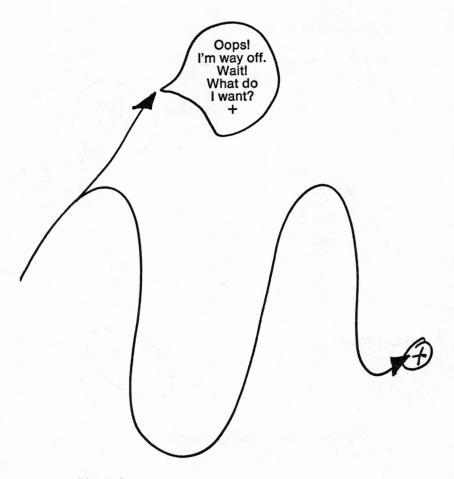

I like to have supporters,
cheerleaders,
along the way,
who also see me as **+** .

They help keep me focused on
the finish.   **+**
I like to have them cheer and shout.

Cheerleaders are great! I get energy
from them!
I *know I can* when I hear them cheer!

I'm usually tougher on me than you are.

Sometimes I find myself losing my **+** image.
I switch over to a **−** image instead.
I start seeing myself as falling behind,
off course.
I start thinking I can't do it.

I don't keep cheering myself on.

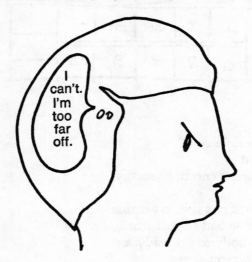

I become a cheer-less leader for me.

I can't do it.
I feel too tired.
I think I'm just not good enough.
I see defeat,
disappointment,
failure.
It's not what I want any more.

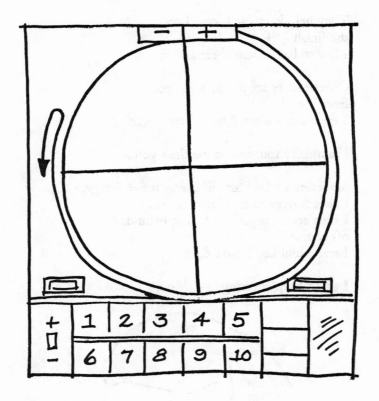

My energy
begins to slow down.
I get tired.
I don't keep generating energy.

I see myself not able to get that.   —
I think how bad I'll feel when
I tell my body to get ready for
disappointment,   —
embarrassment,   —
not doing what I said.   —

And I start feeling
more and more that way,
because I've failed.

My body responds, slouching and bending
under this latest
defeat.

Who sabotaged my image?
Who said I couldn't do it?

I did.
I quit.
I stopped holding that **+** image,
and focused on **—** instead.

And what I saw is what I got.

But I don't like to see that.
I prefer to say it was not me, it was you;
you did it to me.

You didn't cheer enough.
You made it hard for me.
You didn't believe in me.
You were better prepared, had more money behind you,
newer equipment, better luck.

I don't like hearing all that,
but when I'm really honest I remember
how I chose to let go of my **+** image,
how it got too hard,
and I decided I couldn't, so . . .

it was safer, smarter for me
to let that image go,
to accept defeat.

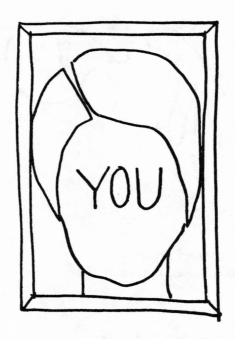

That's when I really use you as a
mirror of me.

I see reflected in you the parts of me
I prefer not to see in me.

I YOU didn't cheer enough.
I YOU made it hard for me.
I YOU didn't believe in me.

I can correct these statements
to how it really was,
replacing YOU with I.
You were better prepared,
had more money behind you,
newer equipment,
better luck?

NO. You did more
to bring your + image
into creation.
I gave up on my + image.
I switched to − , and that is what I got!

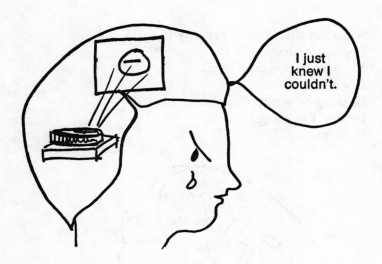

Sometimes it's definitely true that YOU,
my outside audience,
say I can't,
that I'm not good enough,
that you don't believe I can.

But when I'm seeing everything *positively*
within me,

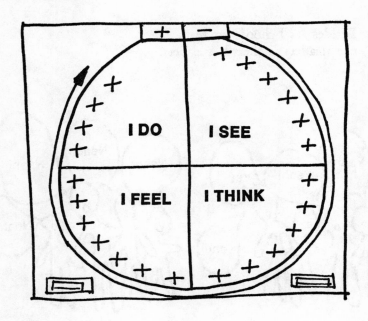

when I'm *clear*, I'm on my way to **+** ,
I hardly notice
I'm not affected by it at all.
I even laugh inside,
thinking how surprised you'll be
because I'm going to do it.
Wait and see.

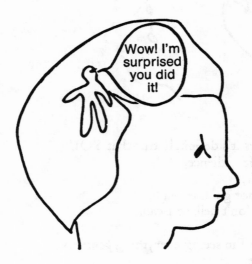

Besides . . . I choose my team,
cheerleaders or cheer-less leaders.

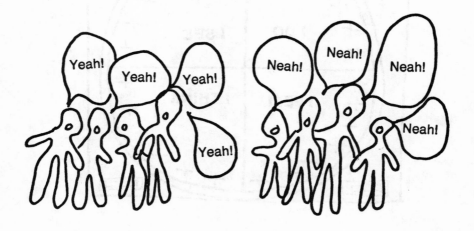

The only time your disbelief,
your lack of enthusiasm,
affects me, is when it *reflects*
disbelief, lack of enthusiasm,
within me.

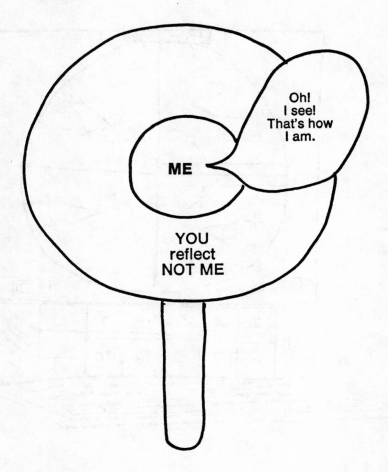

You reflect for me
the parts of − me
I don't see.

You reflect to me +
the parts of WHO I AM
that I deny.

You reflect NOT ME
to me,
the parts I have not yet found,
not recognized.

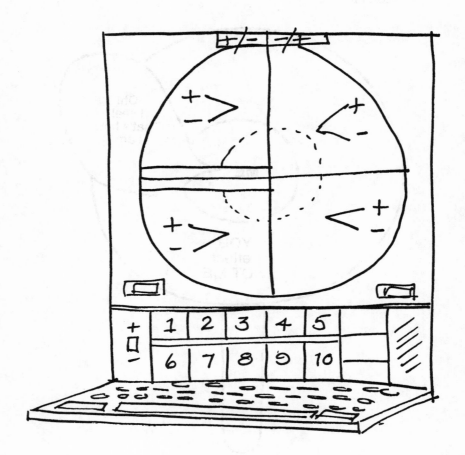

7

Mastering the game of ME AND YOU

Voice: You have spent your life playing the game of separation. Is that the game you wish to play now? You haven't always gotten what you wanted because you haven't known who you are, the wholeness of it, the fullness.

me: Yes. I see now that to be a response-able creator I must create knowing *I am me and you*. If I create operating from a program of separation, I will create separation.

Voice: And resistance.

me: Resistance? I don't understand.

Voice: As long as you operate assuming others are separate, that what you do does not affect them, others will resist you. That resistance is feedback, if you will listen, that you are forgetting who you truly are and who they are. This is an exciting time on your planet. Many of the agreed upon separations are disappearing, the distances reduced by air travel, the lack of communication by radio, TV, phone; and you have been so productive that things are becoming available to most people. There is not such great separation over things. And you are being tested now: am I my job, my possessions, my wife or husband? Who am I really? A challenging question. Am I really separate? Are you different from me? I have tried on many costumes—dressed as a child, as a parent, as a pilot; visited here and there, tried your clothes, your foods, your ways, your systems, and they all seem to be OK, workable for you based on yours. And sometimes as I have tried on your ways, I have found them more valuable than my old ways, and I have made them a part of me. I have done that enough now so that I really know all of your ways are MY POTENTIAL ZONE, potential ways I could be, things I could do. You are all valuable resources to me as I am expanding more and more into WHO I AM, allowing you more and more to be WHO YOU ARE, now loving me and you.

Let's review again the game.

All of you are the missing parts of WHO I AM,
which I have not found, I have not recognized,
which I cannot get close to explore.

And when I see you, I have been
at a definite disadvantage.
Remember the game of separation,
the way it is?

There is the fence,

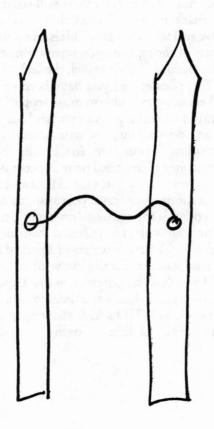

and the charge.

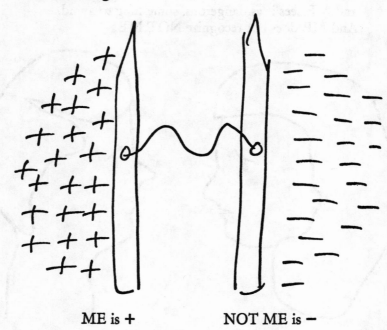

ME is **+**   NOT ME is **−**

ME does not like the ZAP,
and ME sees it as dangerous, something to avoid.
And ME does not recognize NOT ME.

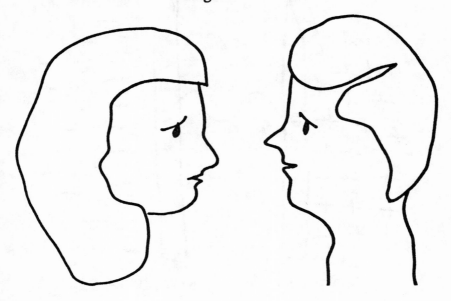

Remember, they haven't been together since birth.
And besides, NOT ME has been re-named YOU,

to make it even more challenging,
even a better game.
But by now ME has discovered
it is an electronic game,

and ME is in charge of the charge.
If ME knows something is missing,
ME can switch MY CHARGE

from − to + , from + to − ,
to take advantage of the Laws of the Universe
so ME will automatically attract what ME wants.

That sounds like it would make it simple
to discover all the parts of

WHO I AM

The Laws of the Universe:
opposites attract, like charges repel.
But *the way it is* is

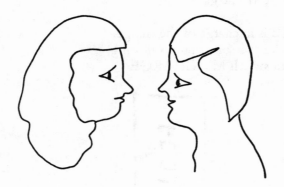

ME sees YOU   and   YOU sees ME,
since the names have been changed.

ME does not know that YOU
are really a part of WHO I AM
that ME is searching for and cannot find.
ME can only discover NOT ME
in the reflection of YOU.
YOU can only discover NOT YOU
in the reflection of ME.

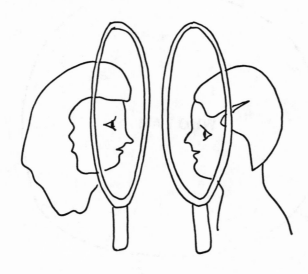

YOU is a mirror for an unknown part of ME.
ME is a mirror for an unknown part of YOU.
But like all mirrors, things are reversed.
ME sees over *THERE* instead of over *HERE*.
YOU sees over *HERE* instead of over *THERE*.

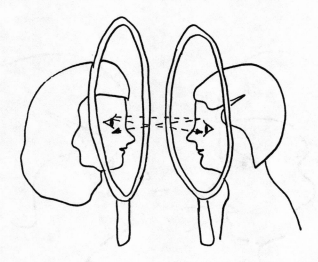

NOT ME can only be explored through communication.
This is another part of the game.
ME and YOU can talk.

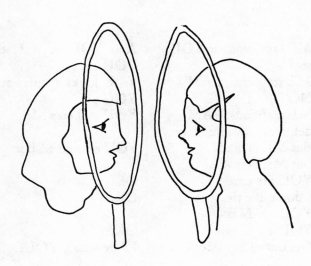

YOU can tell ME what YOU see,
and ME can talk back.
ME says, I can't see all of WHO I AM.
What do YOU see?
YOU says, I can see YOU.

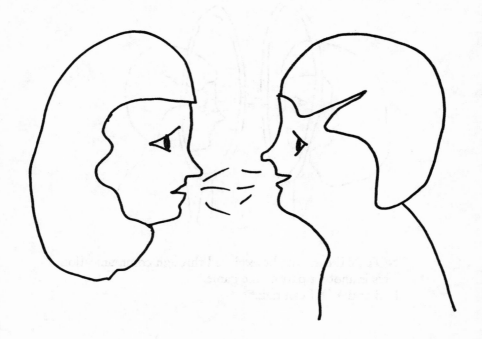

ME says, what do YOU
see?
ME responds, I AM
NOT.
ME responds, I AM
definitely *not* like that.
But ME is mad.
But ME is mad.
YOU are crazy.
I don't like the way
YOU see ME.
YOU are blind.
Get out of my sight!

And YOU says, I see
YOU are . . . .
YOU looks again. I see
YOU are . . . .
YOU still sees ME.

YOU is confused, but . . .

OK.
OK.

OK.
I'll be seeing YOU.

Or YOU can get mad too, and
ME will have to defend *MY SYSTEM*.
YOU will have to defend *YOUR SYSTEM*,
each feeling attacked
by the other.

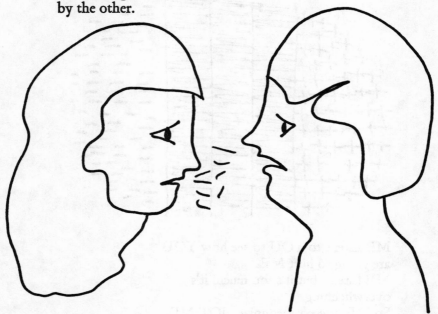

ME sees YOU, and YOU sees ME.
ME won't listen to YOU.
ME doesn't believe YOU.
ME has gotten ZAPPED by YOU before
and doesn't want to get ZAPPED again.

ME builds up the charges even more.

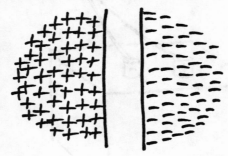

ME hates YOU!

ME needs insulation. ME has to protect ME
from YOU. ME needs *de-fence*.

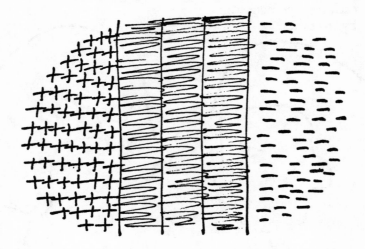

ME listens to YOU to see how YOU
are going to hurt ME.
ME listens, but it's too much, it's
overwhelming.
So ME doesn't recognize NOT ME,
doesn't remember that YOU are part of WHO I AM.

And every time ME gets up the nerve
and gets close,
YOU ZAPS ME.

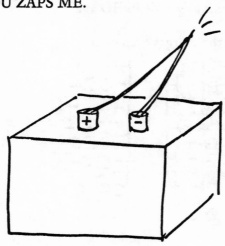

So ME was right.

YOU are dangerous.
That is how ME sees YOU.
ME does not even get near YOU anymore,
so ME's chances of finding more parts
of WHO I AM are
really reduced.

ME is separate-d
from YOU.

But something new has happened.
ME has learned that
ME is the one *in charge*.

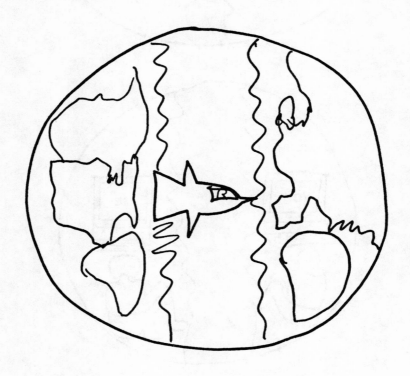

ME can fly over the distance to YOU.
ME doesn't have to get close to communicate.

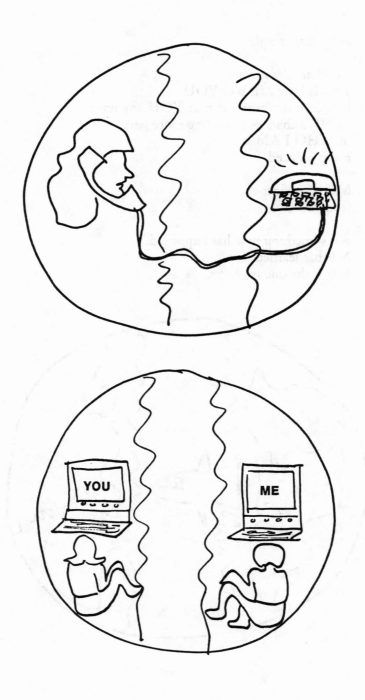

ME sees YOU   YOU sees ME.

It is safe.
ME knows that there are some things
ME CAN'T   but YOU CAN.

How does ME get YOU to do what ME can't do?

But ME has played this game before.
ME knows from experience that
if ME sees YOU as better than ME,
ME will be scared.
ME will be afraid to ask for what ME wants
for fear YOU won't like ME and YOU will leave.
So ME does what YOU wants instead of asking.
ME doesn't feel like ME with YOU,
so ME eventually leaves YOU.

ME has seen it played the other way too.
If YOU sees ME as better than YOU,
YOU will need ME
and YOU will be scared.

YOU will be afraid to ask for what YOU want
for fear ME won't like YOU and leave YOU.
So YOU do what ME wants instead of asking.
YOU don't feel like YOU with ME,
so YOU leaves ME.

ME knows from memory that neither of those programs
produces what ME wants.
ME has updated MY program
deleting those methods,
for ME knows their results.

ME must spend a lot of MY time and MY energy,
and YOU must spend a lot of YOUR time and YOUR energy
re-inforcing the de-fences,
charging the sides,
insulating and re-insulating

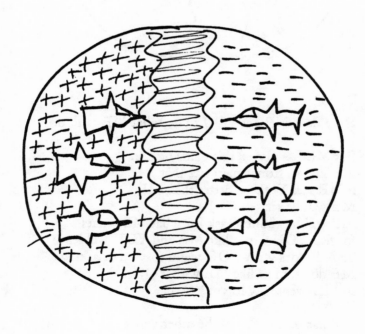

to protect ME   from YOU.

And this is where ME and YOU are in the game.
The physical universe is a great teacher.
The law is

+ attracts −
− attracts +
+ repels +
− repels −
more attracts less
less attracts more.

It set up to get ME moving—
      I WANT is attracted to I'VE GOT,
        I'VE GOT is attracted to I WANT—
and keep ME moving—
        I'VE GOT repels I'VE GOT,
          I WANT repels I WANT.
The physical universe is set up to get
          ME   and   NOT ME
          +   −
                    together.
ME has charged the parts of WHO I AM.
ME has said,
I want to be ME + . . . NOT YOU − .
I like ME + . . . NOT YOU − .
I like what I have.
But wait.
Sometimes ME sees what ME doesn't have
is better than
what ME has.
I WANT THAT.   +

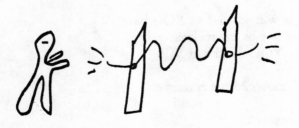

ME is still afraid,
but ME knows
that the ZAP is a signal
to be alert,
for discovering a missing part.

ME has a CHOICE.

ME can just keep seeing what ME wants +
that looks good,
that really looks good.

Then ME is naturally attracted to YOU + ,

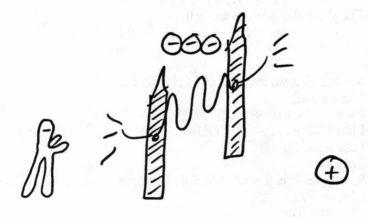

or ME can see how scary the fence is.

ME can charge up the fence.

ME sees how much *de-fence* YOU have,
how many bombs and rockets,
how much YOU could hurt ME.

And ME knows ME is in charge.

ME is the parent.

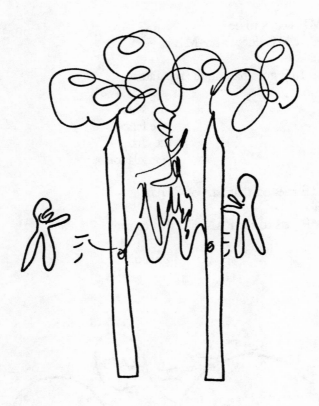

ME is the child

ME is the projectionist.

ME is the programmer.

ME has explored and discovered
many parts of YOU,
of NOT ME.

And with ME getting closer to YOU
to get what YOU have,
sometimes ME sees
YOU have a part
I would like to have in ME.

ME wants to be
what ME doesn't see ME is.

So ME goes past all the separators,

               the space,
               the fence,
               the charge,
               the insulation.

ME tries on that part of YOU
till
ME gets to see I AM like that too.
                    −   +
                neutral

Yes, ME says,
I AM LIKE THAT TOO.
ME has used YOU,
YOUR REFLECTION,
to recognize another missing
part of

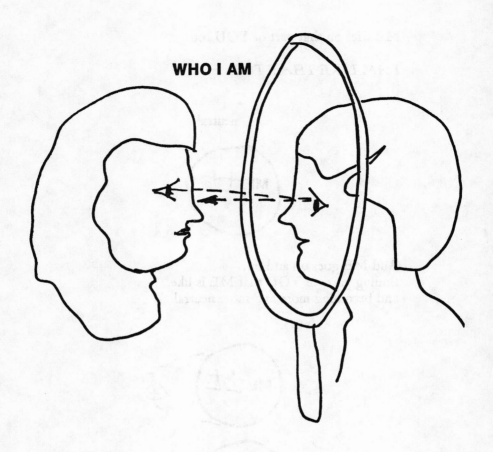

Then ME +/− looks to see what else
ME is NOT like,
for another *part* of NOT ME.
ME says,
I AM not like YOU.
I would like to be like YOU.

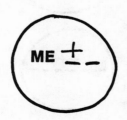

ME tries on that part of YOU too.

I AM LIKE THAT TOO.

And ME goes on and on,
finding parts of YOU that ME is like,
and becoming more and more neutral.

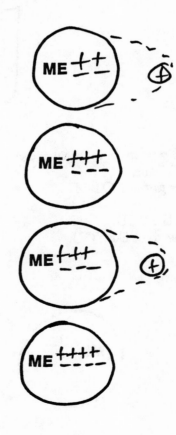

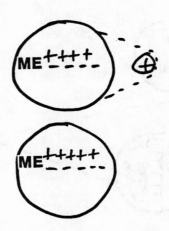

And this is how the game is played.
    I don't have that.   —
    I want that.   +
    I've got that. I'm neutral.   −/+
    I'm not like that.   —
    I want to be like that.   +
    I'm like that too. I'm neutral.   −+/−+
    I don't have that.   —

Sometimes it is *something*
I say I don't have.

Sometimes it is *someone*
I say I'm not like.

So I am attracted to those parts that
I say I am missing.
I AM IN CHARGE OF THE CHARGE.
As long as ME sees ME as lacking,
as long as ME knows something is missing,
NOT ME will be attracted to ME.

That's MY INTERNAL GUIDANCE SYSTEM at work.
It is the Law of the Universe.
The physical universe is a great teacher,
a silent supporter.

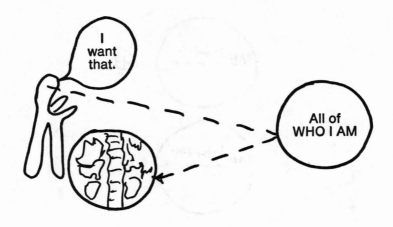

But why isn't it all *neutral* now?
All the +es attracted to all the −es,
all the −es attracted to all the +es,
all the +es repelled by all the +es,
all the −es repelled by all the −es,
more attracted to less,
less attracted to more.

It looks like such a perfect game!

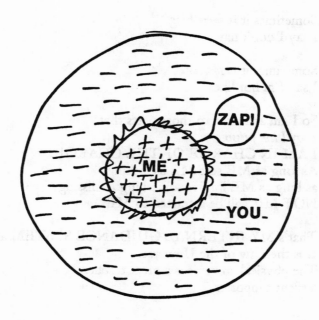

Because
I have separated ME from YOU,
I have put distance between us,
time and space.
I have built up de-fences between us.
I have insulated ME from YOU,
not risking communications between us,
afraid YOU would hurt ME,
MY feelings.

Voice: That's how it has been so far.
Look at your viewer again, at your creative
circuit.
YOU are the programmer in charge, and based
on what new input YOU have now,
how do you need to update your old program?

me: I was afraid. I spent most of my time worrying
about YOU, what YOU would do
to prevent ME,
to hurt ME,
to take away what I want,
to make ME, MY SYSTEM, wrong.
I decided I had to do that so long ago,
it's a habit now.

Voice: Yes, a habit of creating.
What was the major image YOU held?
The major underlying statement in your program
that you operated your life from?

me: That I am ME, not YOU.
That I must protect ME from YOU.
That I must be on guard, keeping up
my fence, keeping ME safe from YOU.

And, oh yes, of course, that YOU are dangerous.

Voice: Good. YOU see that now.

me: I have operated my life from behind my fence
since almost the very beginning.
That's really how I've seen it, my view,
my system, isn't it?

Voice: Yes. Look closely. You're seeing something
that has been *behind your eyes* till now.
Something you've never really seen.
Your most basic operating assumptions
are behind your eyes. You view the world
through those assumptions.

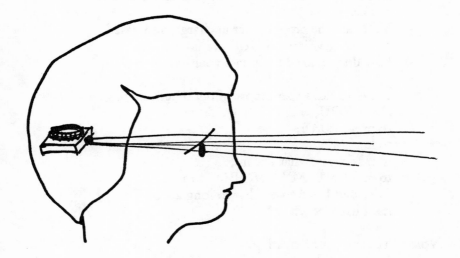

So then, of course, you always see it that way.
It makes it very difficult to notice that
you are, in fact, the projectionist.

me: Yes, I'm beginning to see a lot more about me
as the creator of my world.
I'm able now to see and hear those images on
my internal screen, my own soundtrack,
what I say to me as I think.
I see how I create my feelings, how I decide
what to do and what not to do,
how I react* to the world.

---

* *Interesting word, re-act. Dictionary says* "to return to a former condition."

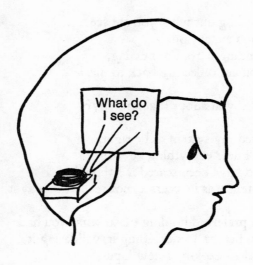

My old strategy was
I look at you,
I see you, then
I decide
what that means.
I tell myself things from *within my system,*
about what I see *outside my system.*

I *impose** my system on your system,
all of your systems,
on the world,
where it does not apply.

My system applies only to ME.
I see that now.

Voice: So were you really interested in their systems,
how they saw you?

me: Well I thought so. But it seems to me now that
what I saw inside,
what I said inside,
was much more important to me

* *Interesting word,* im-pose, *to put on; an imposition, a burden placed on another.*

than finding out what you are seeing,
what you are saying,
than finding parts I'm missing,
that you are reflecting back to me.

Voice: Why did you adopt that strategy?

me: I wanted my system to be right.
I felt I knew everything already.
I would have been scared if I thought
my system was inaccurate, not really the way it is.

Voice: So you preferred holding on to what you had
decided before, to defending it, validating it,
rather than exploring new input,
new data,
expanded information.

me: Yes, I did.
I always compared whatever new I saw with
my old system.

Voice: And what happened if they didn't agree?

me: Oh, I see. I chose to trust my old program
rather than to update it to include
current data and experiences.
I have not been a very efficient programmer.

Voice: Yes, and that's why it was so hard for you
to allow others' points of view about you.
You were attached to your old program,
to the past.

You were caught within the limits of
your old program.

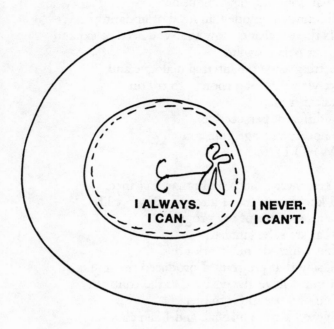

I ALWAYS.
I CAN.

I NEVER.
I CAN'T.

me: I really see, I feel sad about . . . .
but I really preferred my system
to being with you and exploring your system,
your point of view about WHO I AM.
And I've spent a great deal of my energy
and yours defending my internal view
from your external view.

Voice: What are you hearing you say to you?

me: Oh yes, those old familiar soundtrack excerpts:
No, I'm really not;
No, I didn't mean;
No, I didn't say;
No, I didn't do;
No, I didn't think;
No, you don't understand me.

Voice: Yes, good. Is there a chance now that
your reflectors might be accurate,
up to date,
that your old view might be
limiting, outmoded, in need of updating?
Is there a chance now that you need to expand
your ME outward,
setting aside the internal dialogue and
re-viewings long enough to try on
another view,
a different perspective,
another vantage point on
WHO I AM?

me: Yes, there's much more than a chance.
I know now that I am operating my life
with sections of my program
that are safe, familiar,
but which do not work now.
Using that program, I produced the results
I got. I have always been at the controls.
No one else did it to me.
Now I have a manual, and I can choose
to set a new course,
using my creative energies effectively
to get what I want now,
I can *complete* or *delete* my old pile of
incompletions.
I can choose where I have resistance,
freeing my energy for what is new,
committing and updating,
doing whatever it takes.
I have the ability now to operate
at *full power*,
to *master the game*.
I know WHO I AM and the purpose of the game.
And I can use that,
along with the laws of the universe,
to my advantage,
seeing what I want,
saying, thinking what I want,
feeling what I want,
doing what I want,

not merely seeing what I saw before,
saying what I've said before,
doing what I've done the way I've always done it.
It is a *new* game, an exciting one,
one I choose to play
for me and for you,
knowing that is
WHO I AM.

Voice: Yes. And how have others responded to your
old strategy?

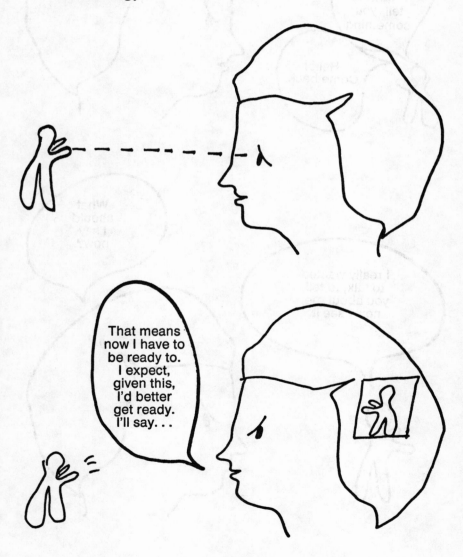

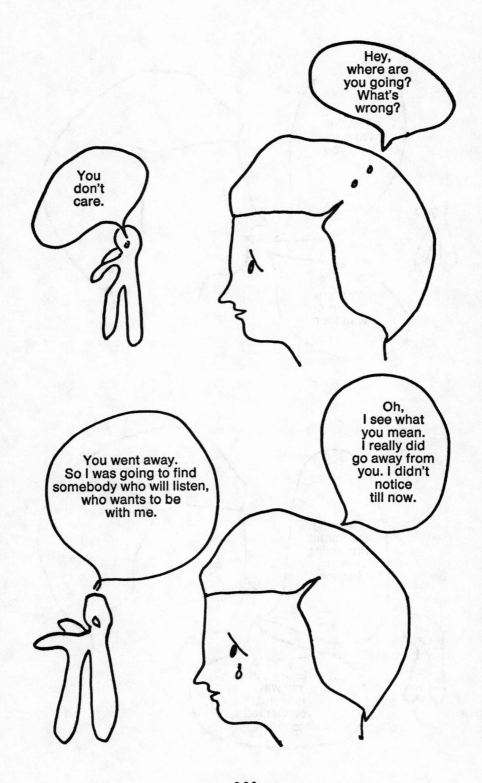

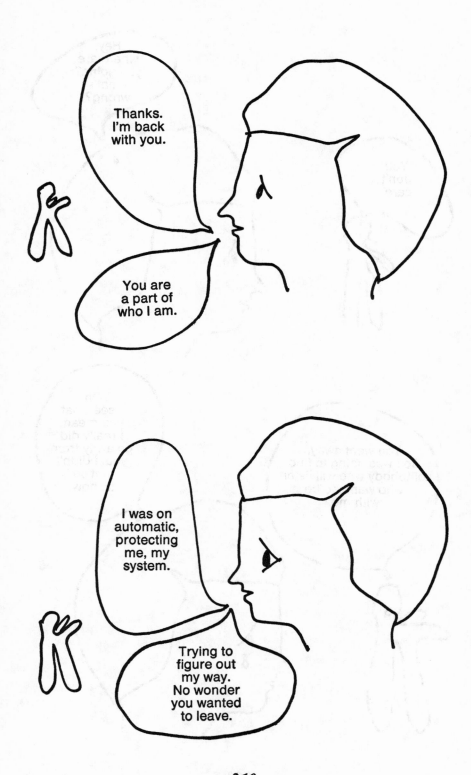

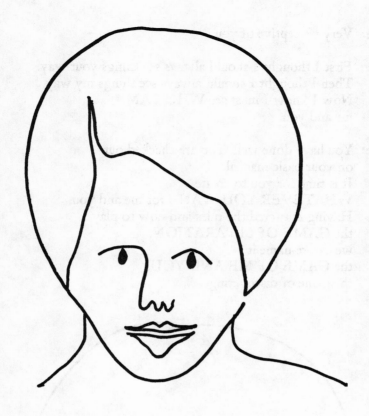

me: I wonder how often I've done that
with you.
I'm sorry.
Please forgive me
for not really being interested in you.
I am going to be with you
when I'm with you.
I'll have plenty of time to be with me,
to look and listen to my system
when you're not sharing with me
about the parts I don't notice.
I can ask you questions about your point of view.
You know, I get scared being with you fully.
I'm so used to thinking, getting ready for,
rehearsing.
It's a habit I'm going to update.

Voice: Very perceptive of you.

me: First I thought I should always see things your way.
Then I thought I should always see things my way.
Now I know I must see WHO I AM,
me and you.

Voice: You have done well. You are checked out
on your basic manual.
It is time for you to create
WHATEVER YOU WANT for me and you.
Having mastered the rules and how to play
the GAME OF SEPARATION,
we can re-name it
the GAME OF ME AND YOU,
the game of discovering

The GAME OF BEING *HU MAN**

* *Interesting word*, hu man, *GOD man.*